THE MAN BEHIND THE CURTAIN

A BACKSTAGE ADVENTURE INTO **CHRISTIAN THEATRE** WORLDWIDE

RICHARD MONTEZ

This memoir is a truthful recollection
of actual events in the author's life.
The chronology of some events has been compressed.
Some conversations have been recreated or altered.
When necessary, the names and identifying characteristics
of individuals and places have been changed
to maintain anonymity.

to Viviana

THANK
YOU

During the pandemic of 2020, I thought, *I've journaled all my life. Putting a book together should be a piece of cake.* Almost two years later, I have a new appreciation for authors who have chosen to maneuver a small vessel, their story, through a tempestuous ocean of words, squalls, and storms.

To Guy Brooke, thank you for patiently encouraging me to move forward despite my hectic show schedule to write this book. Your ideas and gentle nudges have brought this project to a finish. You have braved the storms of my ramblings, fought through the dark caves of my grammar, slashed and trashed through the jungles of run-on sentences, and led me to the summit.

To my team at Cornerstone, Paul and Brenda Platt, Bryan and Robyn Adams, Paul and Rose Grayburn, Stacy Muth, Lori Kooiman: I am so grateful to you for helping me carry this message of hope around the world through your vision, prayers, and your love for me. I'm eternally grateful. Together, we'll continue reaching the nations with the glorious gospel of Jesus Christ.

I save the best, my favorite, for last. To my Lord and Savior, Jesus Christ, for the incredible sacrifice You endured so that I might have life. You are the cornerstone on which Cornerstone Theatre is built. I dedicate my life and this book to You.

ENDORSEMENTS

Richard Montez is a unique man. His ability to stage high-level theatrical productions in a limited time, with limited material and limited artistic resources, is simply stunning, as well as his passion for using them to preach the gospel worldwide. I was privileged to experience many such miracles. The very way we met was a miracle itself. Several months after I visited Korea in 2005, a stranger whom I met there by pure accident sent me a note asking if I wanted to meet Richard. Via the Internet, we agreed to meet in Croatia. I asked him where his theatre was located, and he said we'd make one together in Croatia. I had no idea what that would mean, but it was the beginning of an ongoing friendship and many adventurous years that greatly influenced my life and tens of thousands of people all over Croatia and the neighboring countries. Working with more than 1000 volunteers and fifty professional artists in twenty cities gave us the unique opportunity to introduce them to Jesus even by praying during rehearsals. For some, this was so unusual that it occasionally brought funny reactions. Through Richard's persistence to keep God in the center of every production, national celebrities began to take part in these unusual habits of thanking God in all we do. It reminded me how important it is to bring God to the people in the arts and in show business. We would never have had this opportunity in Croatia if this stranger in Korea had not introduced me to Richard and Cornerstone Theatre.

—Vlado Hoblaj
Pastor, Baptist Church
Mursko Središće, Croatia

Any mention of the name Richard Montez and Cornerstone's productions will bring smiles to many faces. The shows that Richard and his ministry bring are very Bible-based, highly theatrical, and deliver the message and gospel of salvation vividly!

Because of Richard's ministry, a whole section of the church managed to find where they fit ministry-wise as they used their God-given talent to bring people to Christ. Cornerstone has helped us reach out to a segment of the society that has been aloof for a while. Thank you, Richard Montez and Cornerstone Theatre, for twenty-three years of wonderful ministry with us and for your total dedication to the cause of Christ!

—Henry Madava
Pastor, Pobeda Church, Kyiv, Ukraine

Without a doubt, in twenty-five years of ministerial life, one of the most momentous moments has been meeting Richard Montez, director of Cornerstone Theatre. That was the beginning of a new stage for my leadership and for the church of the Carabayllo district, one of the most marginal districts of Lima, Peru. Thanks to the staging of a professional theatrical production, for the first time in the history of the church in Carabayllo, ordinary people were taught that they could do extraordinary things. It transformed the limited way of seeing things both in myself and in the team of pastors that we had the privilege of participating, for which we are very grateful to God and to the instrument that He used, Cornerstone Theatre. We've continued to do other productions since, with great success.

—Edilberto Miranda
Pastor, Cristo Vive Para Las Naciones, Lima, Peru

Richard is one of the most incredible people I have ever met. I am so blessed that he has done shows with me all over the world for the last twenty-one years! He's an absolute genius at what he does, but more than his excellence at his craft, I admire his commitment to God! Every time I think of Richard, I go back to the time he spent over a month in jail in Moldova because he refused to renounce his faith. Many people talk, but Richard lives the conviction of his words.

—Marc Accetta
Founder, Marc Accetta Seminars
Dallas, Texas, USA

I first met Richard in 2004 in Seoul, Korea. Over the years, I have seen how his life is like the book of Acts. I have personally seen how the Lord protected, provided, and opened doors for him. Richard could've been successful, famous, and rich, but he denied his dreams to follow Jesus. The church I pastor decided to invite Richard. He didn't ask for compensation for his air ticket, meals, or transportation, and in fact, he provided the music and costumes as well as trained our church members to act. We weren't sure we could do this, but under Richard's direction, we did it! The show was powerful. Surprisingly, 30 percent of the audience raised their hands to receive Christ as their Savior. During the show, some of the audience cried. I have never seen anything like this. Afterward, our church members were filled with faith and were proud of each other. We were now sure that we could do anything in Christ. May the Lord be glorified through His faithful servants like Richard.

—Jung Jae Won
Pastor, Sumgineun Presbyterian Church
Seoul, South Korea

Being able to make professionals out of novices is a God-given gift that Richard has in abundance. It was a great privilege and pleasure for my late husband and me to host Richard for several superb productions at our campus in Port Elizabeth, touching many people with the good news in a totally different way. We love watching plays on Broadway and West End, but this is just for the privileged few. Having productions as good as those right in our building brought the arts to ordinary and underprivileged people who had never experienced something of this caliber before. It brought hope that ordinary people could become extraordinary and change their world.

—Mariana Crompton
Co-Pastor, Word of Life Christian Centre
Port Elizabeth, South Africa

TABLE OF CONTENTS

FOREWORD

It is my honor to write the foreword for Richard Montez's book. As an ardent director, imaginative artist, and inspired singer, Richard Montez has been spreading the gospel through his artistic talent. I thank God for inspiring him to reach people by showing them the love of Jesus through theatrical productions.

He has had several involvements with our church, Yoido Full Gospel Church, and Hansei University in South Korea. As he already wrote in his book, he had a good relationship with the late Rev. Dr. David Yonggi Cho. In 2004, Mr. Montez and his team were invited to perform *The Promise*, one of the most popular Christian musicals in the world. After the show, Rev. Cho invited him to sing a song in the Sunday worship service, which accelerated Montez's continuous relationship with and performance in South Korea.

The Bible tells us that various artists dedicate themselves to God's work. Bezalel and Oholiab made all the artistic designs for God's tent (Exodus 31:2, 6), and King David and all Israel were dancing with shouts and the sound of trumpets when bringing up the ark of the Lord to Jerusalem (2 Samuel 6:15–16). I believe God still colors the world with His artistic men and women, such as Richard Montez.

I hope his book deeply inspires more people to preach the gospel all over the world through their talents.

—Rev. Dr. Younghoon Lee
Senior Pastor, Yoido Full Gospel Church
Seoul, South Korea

A NOTE FROM THE AUTHOR

Dear friend,

As I traveled the open road, I've told friends a story or two from my journeys. More often than not, they'd respond by asking, "Hey, have you ever thought of writing a book?" Of course, I dismissed such thoughts. After a few similar appeals, I put a fleece before the Lord. "If You want me to write a book, I will know it's Your will if I get at least twenty such requests." Within one year, I got over 200 suggestions to do so!

I wondered when I would find time to write. Then, we all learned a new word in 2020: Lockdown. The Lord has a sense of humor. I wrote 900 (yes, 900!) pages that year. However, as my show schedule resumed worldwide in late 2020, I let my book project collect dust. The trouble with writing a book about my life is that life kept getting in the way. The Lord gently nudged me by reminding me through actors and friends who randomly asked, "Hey, have you ever thought of writing a book?"

So I am keeping my promise to you and the Lord. I present to you some excerpts from my journal with equal servings of joy and dread.

I'd love to tell you that I planned my thirty-five world tours from the beginning, but the truth is that it was God moving me forward despite my own thoughts and ideas. As we stumble through life, there is a joy in discovering the rewards along the way. Even if others misdirect us to follow another path, good can come from it, spicing up our life's journey if we remember to trust the Lord.

So I pass that same advice on to you, dear friend: when you find yourself lost on the path that seems to thread through this journey called life, remember it's an adventure that He has mapped out before you.

—Richard

I will not venture to speak of anything except what Christ has accomplished through me, by the power of signs and wonders, through the power of the Spirit of God... I have fully proclaimed the gospel of Christ.

—Romans 15:18–19

THE FORMATIVE YEARS

I was born in the middle of a theatrical play: Mine. The world I saw was a stage, and the people in my life were the actors. I imagined an audience was secretly watching us from behind a wall, a bush, or a car, and I was one of the actors. My hard-working parents did the best they could, but I would've designed a more imaginative or colorful world if it was up to me. Of course, I couldn't help the circumstances of my birth. So I decided to create a world within my world.

We grew up poor in Midland, Texas. My dad worked hard digging holes for telephone poles all day while I watched my mother earn extra money as a laundry lady at home. My older brother and I helped hang the wet clothes out to dry under the hot Texas sky. The little money my parents earned went mainly for food, clothes, and rent. I wanted another world. My desire for lessons to sing, dance, or play piano was entirely out of the question, but that didn't stop me, nor did my overactive imagination.

As far as I can remember, I had a heart for the things of God and for being overly dramatic. I remember dressing in blue and going to church with our family. The whole religious pomp fascinated me: Dipping my finger into holy water, making the sign of the cross on my forehead and shoulders, standing, sitting, and kneeling during the service spoken in Latin, and partaking in Holy Communion all struck me in a most hallowed, reverent way. I knew I was in the house of God. The rows of candles burning alongside flowers before a ceramic statue of Mary while Jesus, suffering on a cross, hung center stage was fact enough for me.

When I was six, I cut flowers from our garden (and our neighbor's), put them in a glass of water, and then presented them with honor, like at church, to a picture of Jesus hanging in our hallway.

Squeezing water out of Midland, Texas, is like squeezing water from rocks, and plants are rare. So my religious flower-pickin' zeal for Jesus didn't go over well with my mother, and she told me so. That's when this six-year-old announced, "When I grow up, I'm gonna work in the church."

One afternoon, while tinkering with a broken glass carrying flowers, I cut my finger. Terrified, I ran to my mother with what I believed to be a gaping wound that would take my life.

I cried.

Mom reassured me it would be fine, cleaned my finger, fixed it with mercurochrome and a bandage, kissed it, and returned to her cooking.

What?

I watched in stunned silence inasmuch as my life was about to end. The cut had to be more severe than that. I could feel the life draining from my body, but Mom was too busy preparing dinner to take my wound seriously. *I was dying. Couldn't she see that? Didn't she care?*

Feeling sorry for myself, I shuffled a death walk to the garden, plucked a precious, thirsty, white Texas rose, and shuffled back into the house. I hoped Mom would notice, but she was still elbow-deep in beans and tortillas. Alone, I lay on my bed, flower clutched over my heart (just like I'd seen in the movies), and with a ragged last breath, I closed my eyes and waited to die.

She'll be sorry, I told myself, tears running down my cheeks.

Five minutes went by. Nothing.

Ten minutes. My stomach growled.

Fifteen minutes.

"Richard, dinner's ready!"

Dinner?

I sat up. My flower fell to my lap, and my feet hit the floor. I decided death would have to wait until after dinner.

My family didn't know or care much about the performing arts. But my elementary school teacher, Mrs. Horn, did. She noted my exuberant theatrics when Midland's Community Theatre advertised the production of *My Fair Lady*. To my delighted surprise, she invited a few other students and me to experience this live musical production firsthand.

I couldn't believe it. It was like Christmas to me, but better. I'd be going to the theatre. I lay in bed at night thinking and waiting. The day of the performance couldn't come quick enough.

Finally, the day arrived. The anticipation was killing me—the theatre! I thought my heart couldn't beat any faster. Mrs. Horn picked me up at our home. I may not have had the best clothes to wear, but I had the best-ironed clothes in the theatre. Mom made sure of that.

The night was warm, and the theatre looked like a castle out of a fairy tale where knights in shining armor sipped cocktails, nibbled on finger foods, and talked about grand topics too important for a seven-year-old to understand. Inside, the carpet ran red to the expansive stage where the pit orchestra filled the auditorium with random sounds of instruments warming up.

I could sense the excitement. Even the smell of the room lingered in imaginations gone wild. I was in heaven, and the show hadn't even started yet.

The overture heralded the beginning of the musical as the hall lights went down. I could literally see the air in the theatre sparkling! As the overture ended, the orchestra crescendoed with the curtain's opening. In scene after scene, the stage lights, the music, the costumes, the moving sets, the songs, and the dances were all creatively choreographed on scenery designed to sweep the audience (and little boys) to a different world. To this day, I haven't forgotten the musical that changed my life.

The show was over, and I was back to reality way too soon. I resolved to get back to the theatre, but how? As soon as Mrs. Horn brought me home, I ran into the house and announced.

"When I grow up, I'm going to work in theatre!"

My dad looked puzzled. "I thought you were going to work in the church."

I had to think about that one and watched my dad's brows arch curiously with my answer.

"When I grow up, I'll do both!"

I'm amazed at how God honored my heart's desire. To this day, I work as a missionary in full-time Christian service by directing theatrical productions. Because my parents couldn't afford dance lessons, television became my instructor. Variety shows like Carol Burnett, Lawrence Welk, and Dean Martin were the rage in the 1960s, and I was glued to the set, soaking in every dance step by memory. Then, I recreated those moves in my bedroom's privacy before forgetting them.

At that early stage of trying to coordinate my dancing in private, my kid brother didn't help any.

"Mom!" Ed shouted down the hall. "Richard's dancing again!"

The little snitch embarrassed me. He made me feel I had committed a mortal sin or worse. From then on, I practiced away from prying eyes. I mimicked the dance moves from memory when I took the trash out to a dark alley or brought in folded towels from the laundry line.

Little did I know that watching television programs aired only once would force me to flash-memorize a dance, a skill that would be the key that would open my theatre arts career.

In my traditional Mexican American family, a woman's role is in the home: cooking, cleaning, sewing, decorating, etc., which my mother taught my sister Tina. A man's role is predominately outside: sports, camping, cars, and fixing stuff, which my dad taught my brothers Tony and Edward. My dad and two brothers loved the outdoors. Me? Never! I loved theatre, symphonies, musicals, ballet, and the arts. My father never understood this about me and discouraged those things that pulled at my heart. As disappointing as it is not to have your father's support, I continued to follow my dream.

My dad was a good man. I just didn't see that at the time. Like any father, he wanted his son to like the same things he liked. He had served in US Army and played baseball semi-professionally. I was an enigma to him. Looking back, I suppose his only way of making me more of a man in his image was to be harsh with me, which would toughen me up. That had a disastrous effect on our relationship. All children are different, and this had the opposite effect he intended, causing me to think my dad hated me. He was overly strict, but when he drank, he was physically abusive and sometimes violent, which devastated me. My brothers liked the same things he liked, so it seemed to me that he was more lenient on them. I wore glasses, but on occasion, they'd break when he'd punch me in the face. One time, a blow to the face broke my glasses, which in turn broke my nose, resulting in surgery. He forced me to go camping, fishing, and to sporting events. My brothers loved it. I hated it. In my immaturity, I exasperated the situation resulting in angry outbursts from my father. All of this resulted in me avoiding all activities at home.

———•◆•———

At fourteen, I auditioned for Midland's theatrical artistic team for youth known as the Pickwick Players. Ed Graczyk, a renowned playwright who wrote children's plays and won awards for his original productions, was our director.

Under his tutelage, I learned to act, improvise, stage-manage, and hone my dreadful dance moves into something less like the ballerina hippo in Disney's *Fantasia*. I was around other young people who loved the arts as much as I did, so we worked hard performing Mr. Graczyk's original plays for the community.

Midland, rich with oil and ranch tycoons, has a long history of supporting the arts and providing quality arts education, and one thing led to another for me. The Permian Civic Ballet was on the lookout for male dancers and heard of my dancing abilities through the Pickwick Players. I couldn't believe it; they pursued *me* to join their company, and I did. What an opportunity. With theatre and now ballet, this was the world I had wanted!

I found myself dancing in several minor roles in several ballets. I still couldn't afford dance classes, but I had plenty of cute girls in the ballet company watching me try to dance and giving their advice.

"That's not how you arabesque," they giggled. "And your pirouette is awful. Here, let us help you…"

Yes, I loved this new artistic world where I could throw myself into every event at the theatre. But the truth is that I dreaded going home. At the theatre and the ballet, they accepted me as an artist, plus I could hone the skills the Lord had given me, even in a secular environment.

Throughout my time at school, I involved myself in as many artistic activities as I could fit into my schedule, partly because I didn't have to go home. I sang in all the school choirs and won several singing awards in state competitions. I was also adept at gymnastics, which came in handy when I became a high school cheerleader. I didn't care much about sports, but thanks to my theatre experience, I was good at revving up the crowd.

The school's drama department was always on my schedule. I performed in various school plays, which included, ironically, *My Fair Lady*. My theatre world had come full circle when I performed on stage as a dancer in the first musical I had attended a decade earlier. I was in the dance ensemble, and I fell hard into a love affair with the theatre.

At home, I lived in that other world. A dark world. More and more, my father was against all the energies I devoted to the arts, and he said so. As a child, I wanted to please my dad. As I got older, I resented him, as nothing I did made him happy. He was against my performances and would keep my mom from attending my shows, which hurt me deeply. I lived in two worlds: the beauty and magic of theatre and the hell of home life. I looked for answers at our Catholic church. I served faithfully as an altar boy, but that wasn't enough. I needed help. But who could help me?

When I was seventeen, our high school choir received an invitation to an international Youth and Music in Vienna, Austria. A trip to Europe. *The chance of a lifetime.*

In Vienna, we met other high school students from around the world, including a few students from Romania. And then, I met two influential people who made a significant impact on my life.

Phyllis and Mark were from another American choir. They happened to be staying at the same hotel, so I bumped into them frequently.

A few days into the events, Phyllis invited me to a fellowship in her hotel room.

"A fellowship?" I asked. "What's that?"

"It's like a party," she said.

A party? Cool. Free beer!

When I arrived, I found it more of a disappointing Kumbaya session where people sat on the floor playing guitars, singing, and talking about God. I thought it strange and boring. And where was the beer?

This is no party, I told myself and looked for the door. That's when Phyllis introduced me to Mark.

"Would you like to be saved?" Mark didn't hesitate to ask.

This wasn't part of my Catholic education, so I didn't understand the question, and I must have looked perplexed.

"Do you want to go to heaven?" he tried to clarify.

What a dumb question! Where's that door? My eyes flicked to my escape route.

"Would you like to ask Jesus into your heart? To be your Lord and Savior?" Mark added. "We'll be glad to lead you in prayer."

I tried to be polite. "I'll pray the next time I see you." I moved toward the door.

Mark walked with me.

"But both our groups leave early in the morning for different parts of Europe. It'll be too late then."

"Oh well," I shrugged, "maybe next time?" I slipped out the door and closed it.

Whew—what a religious zealot. I barely got out of that one and left just in time.

The next day, our choir traveled to Italy to perform, then to Switzerland, followed by Germany. After a week, we were back in Austria for a final concert in Innsbruck.

The following morning, I went for an early morning run in the Alps and marveled at its beauty. The air was crisp, but the sun was warm, making for an exhilarating jog as the world woke. Among the mountains and trees, through the ground mist, I saw a person walking my way.

"Good morning!" I said in my limited German. "How are you?"

"I'm sorry, I don't speak German," the young man replied in English.

As we came closer, we studied each other and stopped dead in our tracks.

"Well, praise the Lord!"

Oh no. It's Mark.

"Mark, what are you doing here?"

A grin pulled across his face. "Hi, Richard. We were supposed to fly out yesterday, but our bus broke down. We had to stay an extra night. We're trying to leave today."

He hesitated for a moment. "You know, we were supposed to pray together the next time we met. Here we are, and I remember you promised."

Indeed, I remembered too and knew that God must have orchestrated this unusual meeting. How else could you explain two people with two different itineraries in a foreign land meeting again on a lonely trail in the heart of the Alps early one morning? I couldn't deny God's hand in this.

In the heart of the magnificent Austrian Alps, this seventeen-year-old bowed his head and prayed with Mark for Jesus to come into his heart. I didn't understand everything that happened when I repeated the prayer of salvation, but I did recognize a supernatural effort on God's part to bring about this holy reunion. God wanted me, and He would have His way. And little did I know, I desperately needed Him too.

"If you declare with your mouth, 'Jesus is Lord,' and believe in your heart that God raised him from the dead, you will be saved" (Romans 10:9).

Pickwick Players — Midland, Texas, USA

The Man Behind the Curtain | Richard Montez

DISNEY AND DALLAS

In the spring of 1976, I attended Eastern New Mexico University, where I sang in the concert chorale and performed in operas, musicals, and dramas with the theatre department. I found out that Disneyland sent out an announcement to all the universities across the United States. I jumped at the opportunity and at once recorded myself singing and dancing and mailed the videotape back to Disney. A month later, I received a response—I made the preliminaries. They wanted me to come in person to Dallas, Texas, and try out. I couldn't believe it!

On my way to the audition, I envisioned being greeted with honor.

"Oh Richard," they would welcome me, *"we've been expecting you. Come in, won't you, and help yourself to some tea and biscuits. Mr. Disney will be with you shortly."*

The reality was far different. Behind a table sat two guys looking like they'd rather be anywhere else than there.

"Sign in. Fill this out," the guys at the table spoke their routine spiel. "Take this number and wait over there with the others."

I took the papers and expected to see a few other singers. Imagine my surprise and deflated ego when I turned to find *hundreds* in an auditorium, each with the same wide-eyed expression of anxiety on their face as mine. I sat nervously with the tea-and-biscuit-less others and waited for my number to be called.

Now, I came prepared to *sing*, as the invitation asked. That's all. So, when the audition staff called me in with the first group, I belted to the rafters, "I'm a Brass Band" from the musical *Sweet Charity*, then I was instructed to sit and wait. They called us back to the stage an hour later, where I found everyone in dance clothes except me.

I distinctly thought I was here to sing, so I didn't know the dancing section in the letter applied to me. I resigned myself to sitting in the front row and waiting.

When Bernadette, the choreographer, came out on stage, everyone applauded. After introducing herself, she turned and looked right at me.

"Well," she said with an air of amusement, "aren't you going to audition?"

My eyes went big. I cleared my voice. "Oh, ah, I already sang."

She stood straight, shoulders back, and peered down at me. "Everyone must do the dance audition." She pointed to the stage.

Embarrassed, I joined the others. *Why hadn't I read about dancing in the acceptance letter?* I would have been better prepared had I paid attention. I continued haranguing myself. But God has a funny way of dealing with unforeseen situations.

In my blue street clothes, I stood with the others and waited for Bernadette's instructions.

"Let me show you the dance we're going to learn." She proceeded to demonstrate the routine.

I reverted to the years I watched a dance on television, took the routine to my bedroom, and tried to repeat it from memory. Now at the auditions, I immediately captured every dance step, as if watching a television performance only once, and then sat down in the front row to review in my mind what she had just taught.

"Well?" She interrupted my train of thought, peering down at me again. "Aren't you going to try to learn the dance?"

"I've learned it already," I exclaimed.

That didn't come out the way I meant. Looking back, I realize it sounded arrogant.

Her left brow lifted. "Well then," she called my bluff, "why don't you come up here and show us just how the dance is supposed to look?"

Catcalls, snickering, and mocking broke out among the others auditioning. Self-conscious, I made another awkward solo march back to the stage.

Why in the world did you say that? I berated myself.

Bernadette shooed everyone with a wave of her hand. "Back up everyone and give him some room." Then she instructed the accompanist to play the dance number.

My mind went into overdrive seeing the whole dance. I executed the routine step by step, just as Bernadette had shown.

Mouths opened. Eyes stared. All was suddenly quiet.

I was mortified, thinking I had danced so poorly that no one applauded.

Bernadette looked at me in a different light now. "How did you learn that so quickly?"

I tried not to sound arrogant this time. "Well... you showed us."

Having never taken formal dance lessons, I didn't realize that in typical dance classes, instructors demonstrate the routine in a series of short segments. Then bit by bit, teach the students in small pieces—a slow and tedious process—until everyone has learned the entire routine. Because I didn't know better, I taught myself over the years to study the whole routine at one time, memorize it, and repeat it instantly.

Satisfied with my answer, Bernadette asked me to sit and observe while she taught everyone else the traditional way. I felt vindicated as I watched those who, moments before, doubted my abilities now struggle with the routine.

The auditions lasted for hours as 200 dancers muddled through most of the dance routine. In the end, Bernadette called out 194 names and dismissed them. I shifted nervously in my chair. She didn't call my name.

Am I to stay or go?

"Well?" She looked down at me with her hands on her hips and a half-smile. "Are you going to join us on stage?"

I couldn't believe it—I came prepared to sing, had to dance on the fly in my street clothes, felt like a fool, and ended up as one of the chosen few. I've heard it said, "Cream always floats to the top," and suddenly, I felt like cream.

The six of us gathered and received information about the job's duties—*if* we were accepted. They'd let us know in a month or so.

If? A month or so? What on earth?

My mind wanted to shut down. *Hadn't we just auditioned and proved ourselves worthy?*

The month dragged by, and my anxieties rose with each passing day. The call would come any day now, so I stuck close to the phone.

But the announcement didn't come in a phone call. It came as a letter. I held the envelope for the longest time staring at the Disney logo. I was both excited and terrified. What if they rejected me? What if they wanted me? Pondering the thought was torturous. Cautiously,

I carefully opened the envelope, slowly withdrew, and unfolded the letter. I was accepted!

I shook my head in disbelief. How did this young Mexican boy who used to dance outside in the dark alley without lessons suddenly have a job with Disney?

It amazes me how God uses what may appear to be an economic or a physical hardship to be the very tool for the breakthrough we need. In our weakness, our other senses become sharper. We try harder. We find ways to stand out and rise to the top. And then it occurs to you—God is in the business of making the natural supernatural if we'll simply trust Him.

I had to pinch myself. I was now part of the elite group of Disney entertainers.

We were called The All-American College Singers and did special patriotic shows on Disneyland's Small World Stage in Anaheim, California, five times a day. It was part of a musical extravaganza called *Lady America*, a tribute to our nation's bicentennial celebration.

We also performed on a moving float painted in bright red, white, and blue and built to look like a giant 3D flag. The vehicle and driver hid below and somehow managed to lead the parade safely with us on top of the float, singing and dancing down Disney's Main Street twice a day.

It proved to be a killer schedule between the five performances on the Small World Stage and the two parades throughout the park every day. Exhausting? You bet, but I was never happier in my whole life.

———◆◆◆———

After my time with Disney, I decided to expand my artistic horizon and continue my theatrical career with Lyric Theatre based in Oklahoma City. I worked two seasons with Lyric, signing a five-show contract each year to act, sing and dance in such Broadway productions as *West*

Side Story (in the role of Bernardo), *Anne Get Your Gun*, and none other than the very show that lit this whole acting fire inside me, *My Fair Lady*.

When the last show of the season ended, I left Oklahoma and, while driving back to Midland, decided to stop overnight outside of Dallas. That evening my mind wouldn't turn off. Something inside me knew that my destiny included Dallas, so I prayed for direction. By morning, I knew I should remain in Dallas and make it my new home.

With $200 in my pocket, nowhere to live, and no job or people I knew, I remained optimistic about this new adventure and chapter in my life. Firstly, I knew I needed to find a church.

Lord, please lead me.

I cruised downtown Dallas and randomly asked a person on the street where I could find a church. He pointed me to the First Baptist located in the heart of downtown Dallas.

Day one. I went to the church's main office and visited with Gary, the music minister. He was kind and helped me find a small rental flat above a garage close to the church. The elderly owners wanted someone to maintain their landscape in place of monthly rent. What a deal for a young man! Miracle one.

Day two. God provided me with meals and a job at a nearby pizza place. Miracle two.

Day three. I signed up for the church's choir. I was there more for singing and not for spiritual reasons, but God always knows how to reach us. He knew exactly where to put me to begin His transformation in me.

Soon after joining the church, I learned that Gary had connections with big-name entertainers. Each year he organized a professional show featuring one of them, and this year he brought in a popular personality at the time—Minnie Pearl—and she would need dancers.

Dancers?

I marched into Gary's office, past his secretary, and stood at the open doorway. Before he could react, I spoke.

"Gary, there's something about me you don't know yet." Gary sat straight in his chair, his brows pinched in a concerned look.

Oh no, that didn't sound right.

I held up a hand. "No, everything's all right. I just wanted you to know that I'm a professional dancer. I've danced with Disney and in several musical plays through the years. I'm saying that I can help with Minnie's choreography."

Gary's pinched brows lifted. "Richard. I had no idea. That's great news." He looked past me to the outer room. "Merl, can you come in here, please?"

Merl looked at me suspiciously as she stepped through, notepad in hand.

"Merl, this is Richard. Richard's been a professional dancer and can help with Minnie's show. Can you introduce him to Mrs. Cannon's staff, please? I think we just found ourselves a dance captain." Miracle three!

Minnie Pearl was the stage name for comedian Sarah Cannon. She was a Christian who made it big in Nashville's Grand Ole Opry and television's comedy show *Hee Haw*, and I was about to use my talent for the first time for the Lord on Minnie's show.

We opened *An Evening with Cousin Minnie Pearl*, with Minnie arriving down the aisle in an old jalopy. Her unique entrance kicked off a series of Vaudeville sketches, dances, and Pearl's all-too-funny stand-up comedy routine, ending with her sharing her faith. Performing in the extravaganza and meeting and working with a professional like Mrs. Cannon was a night I fondly remember. Some famous can be born again?

The following year, NBC invited our choir to be part of a nationally televised Christmas special called *A Tennessee Ernie Ford Christmas*. Like Minnie Pearl's production, the show also consisted of skit routines, dance, and Christmas songs featuring a large living Christmas tree holding more than 200 singers. However, on national television, Ernest Jennings Ford sang "Rock of Ages" and declared his faith in Jesus Christ. To a new Christian like me, their fearless faith was like a lightning bolt through my timid Christianity. If they can be bold, then I must also try.

During the Minnie Pearl musical, I got to know the show's assistant choreographer, Bonnie. We also worked together again on the Ernie Ford TV Christmas special. She would later be a key person in my career. Bonnie did the choreography for a theatre group called Incredible Productions. This group specialized in industrial shows for famous companies like Southwest Airlines, Wendy's, Dr. Pepper, and many large corporations. Bonnie referred me to the entertainment company that hired me as one of their professional singer-dancers performing various shows.

Between concert performances and recording songs with the church's choir, I lived my dream as an artist. God opened doors and led me on some unexpected twists and turns in my journeys.

During all this time, something deeply spiritual was happening within me. When I first gave my life to God in Innsbruck, Austria, I returned to the States but had no one to help me grow as a Christian. I predictably stumbled spiritually through my college days and with Disney. But there's a saying I heard a preacher say once, "God loves you just the way you are, and too much to let you stay that way."

When I first started to go to church, my motivation was to sing, dance, and perform. But as I sat in the choir loft listening to the incredible Dr. Criswell preach every Sunday, his sermons convicted me more and more. And to have celebrities profess their faith nationally, I couldn't hide from God or fool my old friends anymore. I rededicated my life, found new friends, made Jesus Christ Lord over my life, and finally, after all these years, got baptized.

Disneyland — California, USA

CATCH
THE
SPIRIT

How can putting God on the back burner be considered spiritual growth? I wasn't growing. Not intentionally. It's not that I didn't love the Lord, but that many exciting opportunities were opening for me in the secular realm. The devil opened new, more exciting doors to entice me to leave behind my newfound zeal for the Lord. The nightlife. Discos. A good party. I explored the things of this world, and for a while, it tasted good. I became the prodigal son of a Father God who was patient and lovingly waited for me. I soon grew disenchanted with the secular entertainment I had loved so much. Instead, I focused more on my daily walk with Jesus. I read my Bible, prayed, and watched for new opportunities to learn more about God's Word.

From time to time, I would drive to Midland, my hometown, to visit my family. My siblings were grown, but the resentment between my dad and myself was as strong as ever. I truly hated my dad. However, as I matured spiritually, the Lord moved on me to forgive my father. When I finally did, it was as if scales fell from my eyes, allowing me to see the actual situation. For the first time, I saw a man who grew up without a father, so he didn't know how to be a good father. Instead, I saw a hardworking, dedicated husband to my mother and a struggling, awkward father to my siblings and to me. That act of forgiveness made me see the situation clearly, and I no longer hated my dad but rather felt sorry for him and loved him.

I decided I'd drive from Dallas to Midland to talk to him, but he felt threatened by me. No doubt he recalled when my younger self told him after a bloody nose, with tears in my eyes, "One day, I'll be grown, and you'll be old, and then I'm going to beat you the way you beat me!" For him, I suppose he thought that time had come. He was older now, and I was at my physical peak. Instead, he'd yell at me from afar. I said, "Dad, let's talk, please." He refused.

After a day, he finally relented, and we went outside in the backyard to talk. He was highly cautious and on guard, expecting some kind of physical or verbal attack. Rather, I said, "Dad, I just wanted to ask your forgiveness for not being a good son to you. I'm sorry."

That's all it took. He broke down crying! My father, the man of steel who had never cried, was broken. After a few minutes, he said, "I was a horrible father to you. I don't know how you could've loved someone like me." The power of forgiveness! We didn't hug, as the moment was already beyond awkward for two men who had only hated each other for decades, but there was a new relationship dawning. Happily, we became great friends over the years, and we made up for the many years that the devil had stolen from us.

In 1982, a few years after I made Dallas my home, a friend told me about Christ for the Nations Institute (CFNI), a local Bible school he was attending. My interest was piqued. I wanted to know more about the things of God, and this seemed like the perfect solution to mature spiritually. I enrolled that December.

First Baptist had laid my spiritual foundation, but Christ for the Nations nurtured my spiritual growth. A healthy spiritual life means letting go of sinful lifestyles and false thinking. The process can be painful, but what abundant, delicious spiritual fruit comes forth when we let God have His way with us.

Christ for the Nations changed my life. The first thing that captured my attention was the artistic side of the school. But the one ministry that pulled at my heart was the school's elite singing group, Living Praise. They were trailblazing new contemporary praise and worship songs and ministering them to other churches and special events around the nation.

Living Praise was a 1980s contemporary Christian band of twenty musicians and singers, all handpicked by the music department director. I was selected as one of the singers.

With Living Praise, I learned the disciplines of prayer, intercession, and spiritual warfare. Through praise and worship music, I realized that there is no higher calling on earth than to worship our Lord and God of all creation.

Confession and accountability became powerful tools. I needed to find someone I could trust with my secret past. My director became the person I confided in and confessed to. He held me accountable under his counsel and direction. I began to heal and grow.

Therefore, confess your sins to each other and pray for each other so that you may be healed.

— James 5:16

In the dorm where I lived, one young man on my floor struck me in a different light. He was quiet and kept to himself. Frank was a nice guy, but he didn't have any friends. I felt for Frank and wanted to take him under my wing, so I purposely went out of my way to say hi and strike up small talk. I invited him to go out for pizza several times, and we'd talk and laugh together. As we got to know each other, I discovered his father was in oil, and his mother was a Bible teacher.

A few months later, Frank felt comfortable enough in our friendship to invite me to meet his parents. He arranged the time, and I drove us to North Dallas.

I assumed he came from a proper middle-class family. As he directed me to his home, we stopped at a large, beautiful wrought iron gate, the opening to a fortress where high brick walls protected whatever was on the other side.

"Wow," I said, "this looks like a nice housing development."

Frank smiled and shook his head. He gave me the code to punch in, and the massive gates opened. We drove into a well-manicured park with gardens, statues, and fountains.

"Wow!" I gasped. "What a beautiful park." Frank smiled again and shook his head.

Finally, we came to a vast one-story mansion with a giant awning at the entrance, the kind you'd find at a five-star hotel. A man in uniform came outside and greeted us.

"Good evening, Mr. Frank," he said. He acknowledged me with a nod. "Welcome to the Murchison's."

I looked at Frank, eyes wide. "This… this is your home?" Frank shrugged. His smile was a bit bigger.

Frank's stepfather is a multimillionaire and the founder-owner of the Dallas Cowboys. Frank chose to keep his father's name when his mother remarried.

The Murchison home and property consisted of twelve bedrooms, sixteen baths, and a six-car garage with white marble floors and red-carpet walkways. The lights and the curtains throughout the house were controlled with a remote.

Outside, we walked around a huge swimming pool with a small island in the center.

I continued my tour. Throughout the grounds, lighted walkways invited evening strolls. Everywhere I looked astonished me.

The Murchison's staff consisted of three butlers (each taking an eight-hour shift to cover the twenty-four hours), two assistants, two cooks, four cleaners, three chauffeurs, one mechanic, one grounds supervisor, and twenty-five gardeners. I'd never seen such extravagance in my life.

I found Frank's mother, Ann, to be a gracious, kind Christian. Her husband was home that evening but feeling sick and didn't come out of his room. So the three of us visited and enjoyed a lovely dinner together.

Visiting with Ann, I learned she was involved in many worthy activities. She held Bible studies in her home every week and was a much loved, sought-after speaker for churches and conferences.

"Where do you work?" she asked me at the dinner table.

"I'm just a student right now," I replied. "It's been hard to hold a job, go to school, and minister with Living Praise at the same time. But I keep looking."

Ann sat back in her chair and studied me with a grin. "Would you like to work for me? I need someone to run errands. You can come in your free time, and I will pay you weekly."

I sat dumbfounded. Mrs. Murchison just offered me a job! She didn't need me with all her servants. She just wanted to bless me. It never ceases to amaze me how God always meets my needs, and I didn't even have to ask.

On the drive back to campus, Frank looked at me. His face was serious. "Richard? Promise me you won't tell anyone about my real life. The one you just saw."

I reassured him. He explained.

"When people know you have money, suddenly everyone wants to be your friend, but for the wrong reason. It can also be dangerous if bad people know who you are."

That explained why Frank kept to himself all the time. He was afraid to make friends. And indeed, because no one knew of his family's vast wealth, no one bothered him. I befriended him because I saw a lonely young man and learned a valuable lesson: love everyone and treat them with respect; you never know what their story might be.

My friendship with Frank and my new job with his mother continued. And being connected with his family certainly had its perks.

I've never been a big sports fan. I can watch a game, but I'm just not a fan. But working for Ann and being friends with her son swept me into their world. Several times they invited me to watch the Dallas Cowboys play live at the famous Texas Stadium in Mr. Murchison's private box seats at the fifty-yard line *for free.*

The family chauffeur drove Frank and me to a special section for the VIP guests, where we took a private elevator up to the best box seats in the house. The view was fantastic! A bartender and waiters attended to us and other VIP guests like the president, the governor, the mayor, and other celebrities, during which their chef-prepared our half-time meal.

I pinched myself.

I continued to be friends with Frank and his mother during my time at Christ for the Nations. And Frank continued to be humble, keeping to himself and living as a Christian in great wealth, but as a hermit. What an amazing yet sad life.

I learned that when we seek to bless others, God will bless us beyond our imagination. Seek God's kingdom and serve others, and you'll discover His hidden blessings are right around the corner.

And we know that in all things, God works for the good of those who love him, who have been called according to his purpose.

— Romans 8:28

In December of 1984, I graduated from Christ for the Nations with a two-year degree in practical theology. The school allowed me to stay after graduation and perform with Living Praise. I decided to live close to campus and my job as a waiter in downtown Dallas. The following spring, the director announced that Living Praise would be going on a two-week all-expense-paid concert tour to—Europe!

I hadn't been to Europe in eleven years, and I was excited to return. One day in my quiet time, the Lord said, "You're not going." I felt His whisper in my soul. "You're staying home." My mind went into total denial.

"No!" I rebuked the devil, holding my Bible like a shield. "You will not keep me from this trip."

Then I sensed God's hand lower my Bible, look me in the face, and say, "Richard, it's Me. You're not going."

I stood at the airport window with a heavy heart and watched Living Praise fly off to Europe—without me. I felt numb and confused. I went back to work that day, waiting on tables and questioning whether I had heard from God.

Obedience can be challenging unless you understand that God is always working behind the scenes. And little did I know, something extraordinary was about to happen that would change my life.

While Living Praise began their exciting tour of Europe, I was bored at work waiting on tables. After the lunch crowd left one day, I noticed a lone businessman still eating in my section. As I cleaned the tables around him, I sang softly to myself so that I wouldn't disturb him. The man perked up and, for a moment, looked my way.

"You have a nice voice," he said matter-of-factly, in between bites.

I needed to talk with someone and walked over to him. "Thank you. I'm part of a Christian singing group." I continued cleaning tables. "I just graduated from Christ for the Nations Institute, and my singing group, Living Praise, is now traveling in Europe—without me."

He acknowledged my predicament with a nod and then asked why.

"I'm still here," I continued, "because I feel like God told me to stay behind. For what, I'm not sure. Cleaning tables and singing to myself, I guess."

His face brightened, and he reached a hand to me. I accepted it with a shake. "I'm Thurlow Spurr."

Thurlow Spurr? *Thurlow Spurr!*

I knew the name. He was a producer for big names like Kathie Lee Gifford, Dino, Bobby Jones, and Karen Wheaton from New Life. He was also the president of the Dove Awards—a Christian version of the GRAMMYs.

"Mr. Spurr," I shook his hand harder. "I'm Richard Montez. So nice to meet you."

He invited me to a meeting that night with other Christian singers he was auditioning. He asked me to learn and sing a couple of songs from his repertoire. After the audition, Mr. Spurr asked how I liked the music. I told him I enjoyed it very much. He then surprised me.

"You've made the auditions, Richard. Next week there's a special retreat for Christian artists in Estes Park, Colorado. I would like you to accompany me there if you can make it."

Would I go with him? You bet I would! What an honor.

Over the three-day retreat, I met and had lunch with celebrity artists like Amy Grant, Sandi Patti, Steve Green, Larnelle Harris, Scott Wesley Brown, producer Greg Nelson, and many others. This encounter was every Christian artist's dream.

At the end of the three days, he sat me down and told me about a particular singing group, the Spurrlows.

The Chrysler Corporation had been sponsoring the Spurrlows for several years. They performed on television and sang concerts at the White House for Presidents Jimmy Carter and Ronald Reagan. And here was this mogul of a Christian producer mentoring me.

The next day I flew back to Dallas. On the plane, I stared out the window pondering the week. I met all these incredibly talented, big-name artists and influential people over a few days. Or had I? And did I sign up with the Spurrlows? It felt like a dream. My head was spinning.

The following week, Living Praise returned from Europe with handfuls of stories about their trip, and I had a few of my own. But would they believe me? I was still having a hard time wrapping my head around it.

In the fall of 1985, I flew to Florida to join the Spurrlows, where I met the eight talented singers in the group. We were scheduled to travel part of the time with another group called Festival of Praise, a special choir of singers from churches around the country. We often toured with them and a live band, bringing people into the presence of the Lord using dance and music.

Almost every night for a year, we were in a different town. Our producer, Bob Pickett, based in the home office in Longwood, Florida, booked us in some of the largest churches and venues in the country, but he never forgot the small ones. Our tour and music director, Mike Mulvaney, presented a fresh set of anointed music at every concert. Both Bob and Mike were also exceptional spiritual leaders keeping us booked and focused on our ministry.

At the onset of our tour, the Lord spoke. "You see, Richard, My obedient son? I wanted to give you more than just two weeks in Europe. I wanted to give you a myriad of tours, national and international... *with pay*."

I was getting to know God's ways. When we trust God, He will bless us beyond our imagination. Indeed, His ways are always better.

CORNERSTONE THEATRE, THE PROMISE, AND SHOW BIZ

f you pull the wick out of a candle and light it, it will burn for a short while before it burns out. Take that same wick and dip it in a dish of oil; as long as it connects with the oil, it will never stop burning. In the same way, we as Christians are the wick; the flame is our actions, and the Holy Spirit is the oil—our lifeline to the throne of God. When we immerse ourselves in oil, we can keep on burning strong and be the light designed to serve God. When I hear pastors or other ministry leaders say they're burning out, I know what's happening. I experienced it all on the road, and this untethered wick was burning out fast because I disconnected from the Lord. I'm reminded in Scripture to keep my roots tapped into the One who gives that light.

So then, just as you received Christ Jesus as Lord, continue to live your lives in him, rooted and built up in him, strengthened in the faith as you were taught, and overflowing with thankfulness.

— Colossians 2:6–7

For a year, I endured the hectic road life. During this time, I burned out and performed on automatic. My mind drifted from our purpose, and I felt my spiritual walk slowly decay. As a person who liked to have things in order, my heart was chaotic. I wasn't spending personal time with God. Worldly temptations still haunted me. I prayed less, and when I did, my prayers were dry and cold. In concert, I wore the mask well, but the truth was that I could hardly worship while hundreds of people at the concerts fell to their knees in brokenness before our awesome God.

I faked my way through the concerts night after night, numb to the Spirit. I began to fall back into my old life in the flesh. Mike saw this and was the perfect friend who gave me the tough love I needed. He sat me down, and we had a heart-to-heart talk. I shared with him my temptations. He nodded.

"God has something special for you, Richard, and it's coming soon, but not now. Not with this ministry anyway." He walked with his hands behind his back in thought. "We all need to mature in our relationship with the Lord before we can minister to others. There's no shame in leaving the group, Richard. We all need to nurture that relationship, and I believe it's your turn to get spiritually fed. Take care of that inner man, and God will lead you into greater things. You'll see."

Spiritually empty and ashamed but determined, I left the road and returned to Dallas, desperate for a renewed walk with the Lord. I felt like a failure. I had graduated from Bible school. I was supposed to be a mature Christian. How could I ever think of serving God if I couldn't put Him first in my life?

"I won't let you play games with My kingdom," I heard the Lord warn. "Either you get serious about your walk with Me, or I will spew you out of my mouth like other lukewarm Christians."

I had loved the Lord all my life, and now that I could finally serve Him full time, I had let Him down. What was I missing in my singing ministry?

Church on the Rock in Rockwall, Texas, where I had been a member for four years, was a vibrant church. Wednesday night, I attended service for the first time in over a year, not performing but receiving. I needed God more than ever. Throughout the service, all I could do was cry—the Spirit of the Lord was moving in me. I repented. I promised God I would serve Him with my whole heart if He gave me another chance.

Sitting next to me, a man noticed my emotional state. After the service, he put a hand on my shoulder.

"Are you okay?"

I blinked a tear from my eye and looked up. "Yes. Thank you."

He smiled and extended a hand with a nod. "Hi, I'm Rich Peterson."

After the service, we talked a bit. He was the director of Cornerstone Theatre, a Christian theatre he had started at Cornerstone Church in Fort Worth. Due to a series of events, he and his family moved to Dallas.

I shared my background as a professional singer, dancer, and actor. He perked up and explained he was producing a Christmas musical in North Dallas. He encouraged me to come and audition. My heart quickened. *Was God giving me another opportunity?* I showed up for the audition, and Rich cast me in his show. A new chapter in my life—a second chance!

My spiritual life soared. Most importantly, I found my ministry niche. This was where I belonged! This was my background. I could feel God's presence again and the joy that went with it. Rich eventually asked me to be his assistant director.

As a result of my terrible relationship with my father growing up, I suffered from low self-esteem. I often doubted myself, feeling I had little to offer. I preferred to serve others, but Rich saw something more in me. Even though I wasn't keen to lead, I had a leadership gift.

Rich is a talented actor, writer, and director and has produced fantastic theatrical works. I met many talented artists during this time as we did show after show, trying to turn the theatre's financial trajectory upward. Cornerstone Theatre was floundering. The success Rich had enjoyed in Fort Worth didn't follow the troupe to Dallas. We moved from venue to venue, hoping for success. Funds were so dismal that I worked as a volunteer while working at odd jobs. I didn't mind. I was where God wanted me, and I was happy to serve.

Then something unexpected happened. Tired of being in debt, Rich announced that the theatre would close. I was devastated. I had just found my calling, and it was about to be yanked out from underneath me.

I urged Rich to continue a new season, but he'd have nothing to do with it. He and his wife were trying to start a family, understandably, and Rich couldn't risk their financial stability to do any more shows. I got it. He needed a more lucrative career to better provide for his budding new family.

I could see how much this theatre meant, not just to me but to so many actors. I pushed Rich to reconsider. He studied the ceiling, then me.

"Why don't you start your own theatre group? I'll give you the name and let you use my shows if you pay off the theatre's tax debt."

Gulp.

That wasn't the solution I was expecting. I had to stop and think. *Could I?* The thought scared me, so I prayed that night.

"Lord, should I?"

"Do it," I heard Him whisper.

"Do it? But Lord, I'm not someone to lead a ministry like this."

"You're anointed to do this, My son—do it."

When I finally stopped squirming, I settled into the idea. I would pay off the debt, and the Lord would bring a new director.

I thought it through and then implemented the plan. I took my little savings, applied for a loan for the rest of the debt, and then paid off the three thousand dollars owed in taxes.

As Rich closed his ministry as mandated by the IRS, I opened mine. I prayed about changing the name, but since Rich had said I could have it, and people knew of us, I decided to keep it. I registered as Cornerstone Productions, the umbrella company for the ministry. I had big plans! I also registered Cornerstone Theatre as the Christian community branch and Cornerstone Arts as the travel branch of the ministry. I had a wholly different vision for the ministry. I didn't want to focus on money but focus on winning souls for Christ. Ironically, by focusing on what pleased the Lord, Cornerstone grew, and we never lacked funds.

Having spent all I had on the debt, I had little to invest in my new ministry; I leaned heavily on God, hoping Jesus would multiply the little I had.

By faith, I announced to everyone our first show under my leadership. We would begin 1988 with our first season and our first show.

We had no costumes, no sets, no lights, no curtains, and alarmingly, no venue.

I made an agreement with the church Rich had used previously to do our last shows together. Since the church only used its youth hall on Sunday mornings, they decided to rent their space to me during the week. After our Saturday evening performance, we had to reset everything for their Sunday morning youth service. I was okay with the arrangement. The important thing was that we had a venue.

We were on our way!

What we lacked in experience, we made up for in excitement and energy that only young actors like us could produce. And boy, was it contagious.

We started advertising on Dallas's most popular Christian radio station and saw huge crowds come to our first show. We reached out to churches throughout the metroplex to bring their members. Churches bused their groups to us weekly. After each show, I announced a need for help, and people stepped forward, answering the call. We recruited numerous Christians from Dallas churches to lend a hand and financially support our new theatre ministry. Cornerstone was growing strong, and like the name, it was a firm foundation in Christ, allowing us to build a vibrant ministry.

We began our second season by incorporating Cornerstone. In the spring, I received a call from my former music minister, David Humphrey, from First Baptist Church-Dallas. He told me about a board of Christian businessmen he was a part of who were starting a new theatre concept based on a musical he had helped create called *The Promise*—the life, death, and resurrection of Christ. He told me of a brand-new amphitheater they were building in Glen Rose, Texas, where they planned to perform this musical every weekend throughout the summer. It sounded ambitious, and I was excited.

"How can I help?" I asked.

"Richard, I heard you are directing a new Christian theatre company. That's great. You know, we're just getting started, and we sure could use some tried-and-proven singers, dancers, and actors to give us a strong talent base. Is it possible that you could send a few of yours our way?"

Of course, I was happy to help and arranged for myself and some of my actors to be part of the original cast of *The Promise.*

We began rehearsals at Glen Rose's new Texas Amphitheatre in late summer. We staged and blocked all the scenes and choreography for the next few weeks.

The amphitheater was an extraordinary mammoth outdoor project constructed under an expansive canopy. On top of a hill overlooking the vast Glen Rose valley, the Texas Amphitheatre sported massive pillars around a hundred-foot-wide stage that housed a landscaped hill of rocks, trees, and a waist-deep river moat separating the actors from the audience. This moat would serve as the River Jordan and the Sea of Galilee, complete with a real boat and a rainstorm. The outdoor seating area comfortably held 2600 people. I had never seen anything like this amphitheater.

The Promise used hundreds of costumes, a 900 light and sound state-of-the-art system, horses, sheep, camels, goats, other creatures, and over a hundred actors, featuring the very talented Randy Brooks, who perfectly played the role of Jesus.

With costumes donned and in full makeup, we were ready for opening night. The amphitheater was packed. We prayed, and as we said amen, the overture thundered through the open night sky.

You must realize we opened this outdoor production in October. Do you know how cold it gets up there?

In the hills?

At night?

In October?

Chilly enough to see your breath! But it didn't matter to us; we were so excited we seldom noticed the temperature. And the audience didn't seem to mind either. They loved the show. Because of the weather, we performed a second weekend, but that's as much as we could do the first year—what a successful show.

The Promise was established in 1989 and is still going strong today. You know God's in it when something like this production has this kind of staying power.

———◆◆◆———

Over the years, as I became known in the entertainment circles in Dallas, I met a talent agent who began to represent me. She expanded my world into television, cinema, and other professional productions. She started me out small, arranging for me to act as an extra in several Hollywood movies.

She assured me that I'd start at the bottom, but I'd work my way up. She was right. I thought it would be fun, but it turned out that I didn't particularly appreciate waiting for hours just to do some mob scenes. I wasn't enjoying the film experience as much as I did theatre, to my agent's dismay. I wasn't interested in being a nameless, faceless extra in films.

I finished the year with Cornerstone as I directed a Christmas musical. The show ran for four weekends and was a success. I now realized another director would not arrive to lead Cornerstone, so it would have to be me. I didn't see myself as the leader, but that didn't stop the actors from looking to me for artistic decisions.

As 1990 dawned, Cornerstone announced her third season. Simultaneously, *The Promise* held auditions in the spring for their second year, and again Promise leadership asked to recruit my actors to participate again.

We were in rehearsals for *The Promise*, and, at the same time, I was directing shows with Cornerstone. The Promise opened their season, a whopping five-month run from June until the end of October. For me, there was little time for anything else. The word was getting out:

The Promise was growing. Cornerstone was increasing, and I enjoyed this beautiful and chaotic time!

Kyiv, Ukraine

THE
BETRAYAL
YEARS

Our fourth season would be successful, but I was unaware of the storm clouds gathering. As an inexperienced leader, I naïvely expected everyone, especially Christians, to have our best interests at heart.

Cornerstone was doing more shows all the time—musicals, comedies, and dramas. Every six weeks, we opened a new presentation, and people around the Dallas/Fort Worth metroplex couldn't get enough of us. The church we rented from noticed that the large crowds filling their church to attend our shows several nights of the week did not return for their Sunday morning services. While they watched, they also schemed to tap into the excitement our shows generated for their own.

In October, after we started advertising expensive radio spots announcing auditions for our Christmas show, the church's leadership called me in for a "talk." I walked into their office and met pious faces staring back at me. The door closing behind gave me visions of a guillotine drop.

"We have decided to end our agreement with you and Cornerstone," an elder announced.

"Effective immediately," another added. "You and Cornerstone are not allowed to use our facilities anymore."

I stood slack-jawed, staring for a moment into the serious faces of the elders, questioning if I had heard correctly. My thoughts raced to understand this sudden ostracization but came up lacking. I'd just spent a lot of money advertising for actors to audition for the show. I scrambled for words.

"But we've made announcements throughout the metroplex. We're expecting hundreds of actors tonight. Can we at least do the auditions the next two nights?"

The elder leaned back and folded his hands in his lap, seemingly considering the question.

"That isn't possible. When those wishing to audition arrive," he reassured me, "we'll have signs alerting them of the change. Goodbye."

As I left, with my mind pounding, I tried to come up with a different venue for this evening's auditions on short notice. But where? Worse yet, I learned that this church had been secretly working on their own musical. They had hung signs alerting actors just as they promised, but not to direct them to me. Instead, the signs read, "Christmas show auditions: Welcome, actors! Sign in here."

They had the gall to glean from my advertisements to trick those coming to audition for Cornerstone into auditioning for their own church's musical.

Fortunately, enough of the actors knew who I was to ask for me when they came to audition. It didn't take long for them to figure out something was amiss. They either didn't audition or dropped out once they knew the situation. These artists informed me what the church was trying to do.

I was devastated.

The following day, I went to prayer. In 1988, I had started reading through the Bible annually by reading every morning (and as of this writing, I'm on my thirty-fifth time reading through God's Word). That particular morning, September 26, 1991, I opened my Bible to the day's reading. I read God's response to this church's betrayal!

> *But now, all you who light fires… go, walk in the light of your fires you have set ablaze. This is what you shall receive from my hand: you will lie down in torment."*
> —Isaiah 50:11

I never wished this church or any church anything terrible, but God's Word was punching back for me.

It was hard to forgive this church's leadership. They callously pulled the rug out from under me so they could profit and build their separate theatre ministry at my expense. They not only devastated us financially but left us homeless with only a few actors. How could they expect God's blessing in their ministry?

This church's betrayal could've been a death blow but for the hand of God. I could be angry or forgive them and move on. I knew that I must keep a pure heart to have God's grace. If Joseph could forgive his brothers over his betrayal, so could I (Genesis 45:1–8).

There is a saying: "When God closes a door, He opens a window." We managed to find a temporary place, a vacant office building, to hold our auditions and rehearsals. A young couple auditioned for the show. I cast the wife in a role, but her husband was a businessperson whom I got to know. When he learned about the betrayal, he told me, "I work as a realtor, and I know a firm that owns an old cinema."

An old cinema? He had my attention.

"With all the multi-screen theatres popping up, single-screen cinemas like this one sit empty. No one's interested. Do you want to come and see if it will work?"

Did God open a window just then?

"Do I want to come, and... are you kidding me? You bet!"

We immediately drove to the cinema. I couldn't believe how beautiful the building was. Outside, graceful arches spanned large columns making the cinema look more like a theatre with classical Roman architecture. Inside, 500 theatre seats adorned the auditorium, with plenty of room for a stage and backstage.

It was perfect.

We negotiated a move-in price of just $1 for the first month! We would be paying monthly rent after that, but this was a tremendous help.

It turned out that this venue was in a better location than the church that had betrayed us. With its authentic theatre seating, the audiences preferred these seats rather than the metal chairs they had at the church. We were back in business with better facilities and a location.

I signed to move into our new theatre home on September 28, 1991, and then invited my actors on a tour of our new home. Standing in the middle of where the stage would be, they looked around in awe. They were as excited as I was.

I sketched plans, and we got to work building a stage, hanging curtains, buying lights and sound equipment, and constructing backstage dressing rooms. We interrupted construction sessions to rehearse scenes and dances, then went back to work, painting and remodeling the lobby. Much work remained to be done in time for our upcoming Christmas play.

The Dallas/Fort Worth metroplex already knew the name Cornerstone, so when we advertised, people came. The other church presented their show simultaneously, which stung because we'd built so much momentum there, and much of our hard-earned audience automatically attended their presentation. But at this moment, I was all too happy celebrating our new home to care much. We had our very own theatre!

I remembered my favorite saying, "You will succeed if you just don't quit."

We prayed out 1991, and we welcomed the new year with a celebration, complete with an evening of formal dance and an awards ceremony. We had a faithful audience coming to all our shows. I had a loyal group of actors, and I appointed council members to help me run Cornerstone.

The following year, 1992, was Cornerstone's best year yet. While Cornerstone started her third season of shows, so did *The Promise*. I had a surprise for Rich Peterson, who had helped me by taking me under his wing six years earlier. I dedicated the theatre to him, calling it Peterson Hall. It had a nice ring to it! I also commissioned a talented artist and fellow actor to paint a portrait of Rich and some of his shows' characters to hang in the foyer. We were on our way.

As word spread about *The Promise's* massive production in Glen Rose, they needed me less, giving me more time to devote to Cornerstone's shows and actors. I was living my dream, happily busy with two growing ministries.

Interestingly, on September 26, 1992, I heard that the church and their theatre who had betrayed us last year were closing for good. I looked at my Bible. It was September 26, 1991, that the Lord had given me the word about their demise. Isaiah 50:11 had come to pass, one year to the same date! I was sad for them but in awe of God's perfect timing.

It would seem that we should be gliding down a smooth road, but instead, we found it to be bumpy with rumor and deceit. A member of my theatre leadership council was secretly causing turmoil.

Although God had called and gifted me for my current role, I had no training in leadership, theatre, directing, design, ministry, or motivating people. No one had mentored me in any form of leadership, thus my reluctance to take the position.

When God calls you, He anoints you to fulfill the mandate He's given you. I committed plenty of blunders along the way, but my heart was then and still is to bring glory to the Lord through theatre ministry.

I led Cornerstone as I felt the Lord decreed, and it was being made manifest. Actors were growing spiritually. Our audiences were expanding. As a result, our finances were increasing. In the midst of this, a Luciferian spirit coveted to rise and take charge. This person's mission was to get the other members to question my authority through a series of lies and well-placed rumors.

Over several months, this one council member gradually convinced many other council members that the rumors he'd spread were out of concern for the ministry. He felt empowered to take the next step and usurp my authority through a process of false accusations and lies. I was so busy directing, designing, and building scenery that I hadn't been aware of any of this.

For my work producing, directing, and developing choreography for the theatre, I took a small monthly stipend of $535. Yet, the council accused me of embezzling funds and hired an auditor. I was shocked and deeply hurt.

The council conducted an independent audit to see how much I was "embezzling."

The auditor considered their accusations, and then he gazed at me. "Tell me, Richard, how do you live on $535 a month?"

"I don't," I said. "I work another job to pay bills."

The auditor narrowed his gaze as if to say, "I thought so."

"Members of the council," he announced. "I don't see any deceit in Richard receiving $535 a month for services rendered. This man has done nothing illegal with the finances. In my opinion, he is innocent."

Yes! Vindicated.

That council member wasn't finished with me yet and continued to infect the minds of the others. I envisioned the Pharisees trying to find a different angle to entrap Jesus. This man was still determined. With a new accusation up his sleeve, he and some in the council confronted me again—this time of sexual improprieties.

Certain members of the council said they had a witness but refused to tell me who the source might be. The devil works most effectively in the dark, and they refused to let this one come to light.

The court of law says that the accused has a right to meet his accuser; evidently, not in this ministry's chambers. They chose to protect their faceless, nameless accuser and instead destroy me. My name and reputation were on the line, and I was guilty in their eyes until proven innocent. Was there even a secret accuser? That's something I may never know.

While I emphatically denied the charges, the council decided to take the matter before my church's leadership. I was thrilled because the church's pastors knew me and had seen firsthand my faithfulness over the years. I had directed shows for the church. And the co-pastor was also one of my past directors from Bible school. He had known me for ten years. Finally, there would be justice.

Or would there?

Two of Cornerstone's council members and I met with the co-pastor. Our council members explained what I was being accused of. I was confident my pastor would bring wisdom and clarity to these allegations and vindicate me of these ridiculous charges. But, in a twist of fate, I was hoodwinked. The clarity I had hoped for only added to the confusion.

"Richard confided in me his struggles back in Bible school," the co-pastor said. "So yes, it's very probable he could be guilty of them now."

This pastor, my former counselor, betrayed my trust and went on to reveal everything I had told him in confidence as a student years ago. Stunned, I felt like I was stabbed right in the heart as a blanket of shame slowly enveloped me as he talked.

I tried to remain calm, but I felt my face flush with embarrassment. My voice shook as I questioned my pastor's decision to expose my decade-old counseling session.

Shockingly, my defense enraged him! He stormed out from behind his desk, fists raised. I backed against the wall while the two council members intercepted him from physically harming me. The blood drained from my face. The chaos at that moment was unreal and unbecoming of a spiritual leader.

In a state of shock, I hurried out of his church office. Marching close behind, the council members separated me from the pastor's continuous rage.

That unfortunate meeting was all it took for the council members to confirm their allegations. They decided to vote to remove me from Cornerstone in the new year. I'd no longer be a part of my own ministry.

My world crumbled about me. I had never felt so alone. This entire attack was one of the darkest moments in my life, and I had no one to turn to but the Lord.

A week after this catastrophe, Cornerstone opened its Christmas show. Since I had been directing this show in the middle of all these betrayals, I would be allowed to finish leading this production (pragmatically speaking, there were thousands of tickets already sold). I was weak and emotionally spent. Mercifully, the council had taken a leave of absence for the holidays. This took a load of pressure off, allowing me to run the theatre and the performances without political infighting. But it was still challenging to lead and direct my cast, knowing that some tidbits of gossip had been leaked. Now, half the cast was for me and the other half against me. My paranoia reared its head; I was sure everyone was talking about me behind my back. Still, we opened.

Thankfully, the public knew nothing of our political drama behind the curtain and filled the theatre each night, excited to celebrate Christmas with us. We welcomed in the new year with the last of our holiday shows and breathed a sigh of relief. The show was a success, but it was a bittersweet ending.

The first council meeting for the new year convened with only one thing on the agenda—get rid of the director.

The council had voted. Upon their first and second motion, the board that I had personally chosen to lead the ministry voted me out of my own theatre. They forced me into a six-month hiatus so they could reform the theatre into their image and then decide if they wanted me back.

I was emotionally and spiritually exhausted. The show had ended, and so had this chapter of my life.

January was a blur. I felt like I didn't have a friend in the world. In a way, I didn't. I had the Lord.

Cornerstone began her sixth season without me. The council would now decide all decisions. They chose their own directors, including those who caused all the problems.

I hated my life.

I would never commit suicide, but neither did I want to live. Daily, I begged God to take me. Now, I'm so glad He said no. He had other plans for that moment. First, He asked me to forgive my accusers. My feelings were still raw, and as difficult as it was, I forgave the council through tears and gritted teeth. I even forced a prayer of blessing over them.

> *If your enemy is hungry, give him food to eat; if he is thirsty,*
> *give him water to drink. In doing this, you will heap*
> *burning coals on his head, and the Lord will reward you.*
> —Proverbs 25:21–22

Lima, Peru

TRANSITION TO INTERNATIONAL MINISTRY

I became a recluse in my own home—not wishing to see or be seen by anyone. I hid from my roommate. Days passed. One day there was a knock at my door.

What trouble now waits to devour what's left of me?

I debated whether to answer it or ignore the persistent thumping. Everything in me screamed, *Go away!* I just wanted to be left alone in my misery to untangle what was self-pity, what was anger, and what was confusion of what, if anything, I should do.

The knocking persisted.

My curiosity gave in. Reluctantly, I cracked the door open. The smiling face of a fellow actor and friend from *The Promise*, Randy Brooks, peeked back at me.

"Richard, there you are. Good to see you, I think? You look a mess. Are you okay?"

I didn't want to rehash with him the garbage I'd just been through at Cornerstone.

"I've just had an exhausting week, and I'm trying to recoup. Feeling a bit lazy today." I swung the door wide. "Come in. What brings you here?"

With a single pat on my shoulder, he stepped in.

"I could have called, but I was in the area, and I hadn't seen you in a while, so I thought, what the heck, I'll give the news in person."

He moved to the couch and plopped down. I could see this meeting was going to take longer than I wanted. He leaned forward.

"Richard, *The Promise*, with all the cast and crew, is having a special meeting in a couple of hours. You gotta come and—"

"Oh no, Randy. I can't commit to anything like that right now. I've got, um, other commitments."

"Like what?" He looked me up and down, observing my disheveled clothes and skewed hair. "Auditioning for an extra in a zombie film?" He laughed. "Come on. Let's go. They need you and your expertise on stage."

They need me?

"Wha-da-ya-say? You know you wanna."

I'm such a sucker for the theatre, and Randy knew it. Knowing they needed my help made it that much more enticing.

"All right. Okay. I'll go. Let me get cleaned up, and I'll meet you there."

Still wary and a bit anxious, I arrived at the meeting. All my concerns melted away when I stepped through the door. My fellow Christian actors welcomed me with hugs—what a balm of healing. I could feel my spiritual blood start to flow again. *The Promise* team did not know about events at Cornerstone. And if that wasn't enough encouragement for my bruised ego, Dr. Ron Corley, the president of *The Promise*, had a major announcement: "A breakthrough, everyone. A couple of years back, the Soviet Union's Iron Curtain fell, and we have just had an invitation to perform multiple shows at the State Kremlin Palace in Moscow, Russia."

Russia? Russia!

My mind jerked awake from its fog, and my heartbeat fast. When I was twelve years old, I gave $1 monthly to Brother Andrew's Open Doors ministry to smuggle Bibles into the Soviet Union. That offering continued and grew as I got older. A love for the people of eastern Europe developed as I planted those seeds. I prayed I would go to Russia one day, and suddenly, the opportunity was right at my fingertips.

We would be one of the first American groups to present a show and the very first to present a Christian musical in a country that not too long ago suppressed religious freedoms. In only a few months, production rehearsals would begin. I had to raise the finances quickly. Suddenly, I had a new purpose and hope. I could do this!

By the deadline, I had raised all but the final $500 that I needed for the trip in seven weeks. I couldn't purchase my airline ticket without this money, due today.

Dr. Corley approached me. "Richard, do you have the money for the trip?"

I saw the concern on his face. "No," I shook my head and mumbled. "I'm still short. Maybe next trip."

Minutes later, he stuck out his hand. In his palm was an envelope. Inside, a check for $500 with a note worth much more. It read, "Richard, you have always been an important part of *Promise*, and we can't do this without you."

For a moment, I forgot to breathe. My lungs puffed a quick breath, and my eyes welled up. I searched Dr. Corley's face and saw sincerity there.

"Dr. Corley, no. Are you sure?"

"Richard, this show needs you. Russia needs you. And if I'm not mistaken, I think you need this even more."

"Thank you, Dr. Corley. I was hoping to go. I'm looking forward to it."

"Well, Richard," he put a reassuring hand on my shoulder, "there's only one thing left to say, 'Look out, Russia, here we come!'"

———— ◆•◆ ————

Excitement bubbled up around the cast and crew as we boarded the plane to Russia. Approximately fifteen hours later, we touched down at the Sheremetyevo Airport just outside Moscow. Despite our apparent excitement, we all would have admitted we were nervous. We didn't know what to expect from a dictatorial government system that was skeptical of foreigners, especially Americans, not too long ago. *How will we be received?* I wondered. If we step out of line with their laws or politics, would we be arrested and swept away forever somewhere in the work camps of Siberia? My imagination sometimes got the best of me, and I needed to reel it in.

On arrival, all 250 of us actors and crew members miraculously made it through passport control without an incident. Outside, waiting to take us to our hotel, were six buses.

I could tell Russians had never seen Americans before, and we had never really seen Soviet life due to their government-controlled communist television. It only showed what they wanted you to see. I would now see Russia with my own eyes. My first visual of life in Moscow was of a man standing on a sidewalk in knee-deep snow, eating an ice cream cone in subzero weather, staring at our passing caravan of buses.

As our buses plowed their way through the snowy streets of downtown Moscow, I couldn't help but wonder if the official color of Russia just might be gray. Gray buildings, gray sky, gray cars, dirty gray snow. Even the people wore gray.

Few hotels could accommodate a group of our size. So we rented a cruise liner docked for the winter on the frozen Volga River. Complete with a restaurant and staff, we had everything we needed.

The next day we arrived at the Kremlin gate. An imposing tower with a giant red star at the top symbolizing the power of the Soviet Union. Before entering the grounds where we would be doing our musical at the State Kremlin Palace Theatre, we each had to show our passports.

It was an eerie moment knowing that just across the street from our theatre was the former headquarters of the Soviet Union—America's foremost enemy. It was now the office of the first president of the new federation of Russia, Boris Yeltsin.

Entering the theatre for the first time took my breath away. The massive stage and ceiling seemed to have no limits. The rows of seats swept far up into heavenly balconies that held thousands. The curtains were also the biggest and most beautiful I had ever seen. The Kremlin State Palace was the country's largest and most prestigious concert hall. It was old but well preserved. We stared in awe at its architecture.

After familiarizing ourselves with the stage facilities, we began *The Promise* rehearsals on stage. We practiced the scene that led to the slaughter of innocents in Bethlehem, as found in Matthew 2:16–18. In the scene, the Roman soldiers (actors) took babies (doll props) from their screaming mothers (actresses) and killed them in an emotional scene. While the scene was dramatic, what occurred offstage was more so.

The Russian theatre staff heard the horrifying screams and rushed to the stage to our aid. There they couldn't believe what they saw: American men with swords yanking babies from screaming American women and killing them. Within minutes, dozens of confused and alarmed Russian workers and security guards surrounded the actors, trying to figure out what horrible thing they had just witnessed. They didn't know the Bible story we were recreating, so we saw genuine concern and fear in their eyes. Besides, we were the first foreign theatre group to be hosted in their hall, and they were responsible for our well-being. There could be no international incidents on their watch.

Our director, Mike, called for a break in the rehearsal while he and our leadership had a lengthy conversation with the Kremlin leadership to sort out this acting thing. At the back of the theatre, we could hear voices rise and Russian hands waving and pointing while Mike's hands pushed the air between them, trying to calm the excitement. Before too long, things quieted down with a few handshakes, and Mike walked back to us, exhaling in relief.

Now that the Russian personnel knew what to expect, they tried to ignore us or roll their eyes at the sounds coming from the stage. You could tell their inner thoughts as they shook their heads—*crazy Westerners.*

For several weeks the show promotions played on all media platforms for all people to attend *for free*. Many Russian people had never been inside a proper theatre before, let alone the Kremlin grounds. This was a rare opportunity for them to get more than a glimpse inside *and* experience an American theatre group performing in one of the premiere theatres in the country.

Opening night arrived. The 6,600-seat hall filled to capacity— and every night following, for all thirty performances. Most Russians had never seen an American theatre group perform, nor had they witnessed the gospel of Jesus Christ. Each chair had a box with an earpiece for audience members to hear the performance in their respective language by interpreters reading the script and following the action on stage. The Bible story suddenly came alive for them with outstanding professional performances that took the people's thirsty souls by surprise. They could not get enough of the living gospel.

I remember the opening night when the overture heralded triumphantly throughout the theatre; I cried at the immensity of what was happening. Not only had the Soviet Union been dismantled, but our show about the life of Christ was about to dismantle Russia's residue of atheism. In the very heart of the Kremlin, where Lenin once declared to the masses, "There is no God," we were now claiming through a beautiful and majestic musical that there *is* a glorious God who loves you and has a plan and a purpose to bless you.

The audience was spellbound.

Each night when the show ended, the people stood and roared with enthusiasm and wouldn't stop clapping until we gave eight to ten curtain calls. Untold numbers of Russians plied the principal roles with flowers afterward, and many came to know our Lord Jesus for the first time. We couldn't believe the response.

After the curtain calls, we went out to the lobby to sign autographs and pose for pictures with members of the Russian audience. From beginning to end, I have never felt anything more satisfying in the service of our Lord.

In between shows we had a chance to do some sightseeing. Next door to the Kremlin was Red Square, the iconic St. Basil's Cathedral, and Lenin's mausoleum, where Vladimir Lenin lay in state. His embalmed body rested within an airtight glass case.

What I remember about Russia and what amazed me was that they had never seen blue jeans. I went into a souvenir shop once, and the shop owner was excited to see the jeans I was wearing and pointed.

"I will give you anything you want from my shop," he said, "for your jeans." I politely declined.

Russians had heard of blue jeans, but there was no way to get them, and here were hundreds of Americans—*all* sporting jeans. Even at the theatre, several young Russian men commented on them.

I also found it curious that Russian street vendors would set ice cream cones for sale outside on a stand, uncovered, in the cold of winter. You'd pay a few rubles and pick up any flavor you wanted—as long as it was *vanilla*.

During our five-week stay in Russia, I became friends with two local guys who worked the lights for our show: Dima and Ilya. Both spoke broken English, and I had a pathetically limited Russian vocabulary. Still, where there is a will, there is a way. Through sign language and drawings, communication was fun. They wanted to give me a private tour of their city, and I jumped at the opportunity and rode the magnificent metro—their subway system where each stop is a literal work of art.

As we walked the streets of Moscow with Dima and Ilya, I was taken aback by the bleak grocery stores. The shelves were mostly bare. You could buy bread, potatoes, vodka or cigarettes, and a few canned items like sardines, but they didn't sell fruit, vegetables, or perishables.

One day while walking with Dima, he suddenly grabbed my arm and pulled me across the street. "Run!" he said.

I followed close behind, alarmed. "What's wrong?"

"Something good. See?" He pointed to a man standing by two good-sized boxes, digging into them. "He's selling oranges. Quick!"

I could see people running to line up for this unique opportunity. We followed suit and waited our turn. There was a limit of two oranges per person, so I bought both of ours and gave Dima my two. He proceeded to peel and eat one, then looked at me.

"Don't you like oranges?"

"Yes, but we don't buy them this way."

"No? Then how?"

In America, we are accustomed to our produce shelves overflowing with fruit and vegetables, not to mention all the other grocery products. It was hard to explain to someone about American abundance who's never seen a Western supermarket. It seemed almost cruel to tell Dima. I thought it best just to leave it.

"I'll tell you some other time."

I shared the gospel with both my new friends. Dima was the most receptive, but he didn't understand who this Jesus was. Cautiously, he proceeded to probe the subject.

"Jesus loves you." I went lightly into the subject.

"Now, who is that again? Does he have brothers or sisters?"

"No, not really."

"Then who's his mother?"

"Jesus doesn't have a mother."

"He only has a father?"

"Um, yeah."

Dima thought for a moment. "So God's a single father?"

"Well, I guess so."

Dima's honest questions took me outside my theological comfort zone. I've always assumed that everyone has a general understanding of the gospel and the Trinity. But here in the heart of Russia, where the government pushed atheism on the people, faith concepts were confusing. However, Dima was sincere and open to the idea. Sadly, Ilya was not.

One day, while I was sharing the gospel with Dima, I wanted to point out that having God in your life can bring you more joy than even your fondest wish. So I started with a question.

"If money were no object, and you could have anything in life, what would you wish for?"

Dima thought long and hard. "Can I have more than one?"

I chuckled. "No. Just one wish."

He thought for a while longer; then, his eyes lit up. "To eat at McDonald's."

McDonald's?

"Dima, no, not like that. Would you want, say, a fleet of sports cars, travel the world, or own a mansion in a foreign country? You know, stuff like that."

His eyes shifted back and forth, thinking.

"No." He shook a determined head. "McDonald's, that's what I want. One day with my family, I would like to eat at McDonald's."

I marveled at his innocent request. Dima wanted the simplest things in life and to share them with his family. Who could ask for more?

We Americans usually dream according to what we consider to be possible. I've never imagined living on the planet Jupiter. Why? It's outside the realm of possibility. Instead, I wish for things that seem possible with hard work and God's blessings. Dima's realm of the possible was to eat at McDonald's.

"Dima?" I put a hand on his shoulder. "It would be my great honor to invite you and your family to eat at McDonald's. My treat."

A concerned look crossed his face. "Richard, no. I wasn't hinting for you to take us."

Still, I insisted, and we set a date for him and his family to experience "the goodness" of Western hamburgers and fries for the first time.

McDonald's in Moscow was a new concept to the locals, and they had built the largest McDonald's I had ever seen. Even the lines to get in circled the block allowing fifty people to enter every five minutes. Once in, I could see the people rush to one of the twenty-two attentive cashiers, who quickly processed their orders. And every five minutes, a whole new wave of excited clients rushed in.

I ordered all of us a Big Mac Meal and a Happy Meal for their six-year-old son. Dima looked around in wonder at the restaurant with a mouthful of burger.

"Wow. American architecture!"

I was a little embarrassed that he would think this was the best America had to offer. He bit into his Big Mac again.

"This is so delicious!"

I wanted to laugh. I enjoyed this moment immensely, almost as much as Dima and his family.

Afterward, Dima asked something I'll never forget.

"Can I keep the french fry carton? And the Coke cup and the burger box too?"

The childlike request was priceless. Dima wanted to show his friends.

"Yes, of course, you can."

"Can I also keep this plastic tray?"

I shook my head. "That, I'm afraid you can't. That's McDonald's property."

My time with Dima and his family was precious. The culture he showed me, the talks we had, and the honest hard work Dima displayed as a light man for the Kremlin theatre will never be forgotten. But the best news of all? Before *The Promise* team left, he and his family accepted Jesus Christ as their Savior.

When our time in Russia ended, Dima became a close friend. He saw me off with a gift—a teacup with the Kremlin symbol embossed in gold and a saucer. I suspect he stole it, as it wasn't new, and he simply pulled it out of his coat pocket. Still, I was grateful. I hugged both Dima and Ilya goodbye.

I left with mixed emotions. An avalanche of thoughts, feelings, and images of our ministry in Russia flooded my mind. God had done a marvelous work with the musical at the Kremlin State Palace, but the real work, I believed, was taking place in my own heart.

I tried to reason through a perplexing situation: How could I continue witnessing to Americans about Jesus when the need overseas was so desperately needed? Hadn't I, for thirty days, night after night, observed thousands of people in the heart of communism, hungry to know more about Jesus? His life, death, and resurrection opened their eyes to the truth of our living God. But there seemed to be no one to teach them more.

Something new stirred within me. A fresh wind of the Holy Spirit filled my spiritual sails. I felt its tug, a current pulling at me. But how or where I didn't know.

The cast boarded the buses, and we all left for the airport; our plane was waiting to take us home. In flight, I reflected on our theatrical production in the Kremlin and how God had moved mightily.

I looked out the window and cried, thankful for five weeks that would change my life and my ministry.

Florence, Italy

A WORLDWIDE MINISTRY IS BORN

I was still on a spiritual high when we touched down in Dallas, but it wouldn't last long. I was renting a room from a Christian actor, a council member of Cornerstone. Upon my return, I discovered all my belongings had been thrown in the garage in a giant heap. My room was empty. My heart sank.

I had just traveled sixteen hours. I was exhausted from the jet lag, so I had trouble understanding what was going on. I was confused. My roommate sat on the couch pretending to read a magazine, flipping pages.

"Why are my things in the garage?" I quietly asked.

"You no longer live here," came the abrupt response.

I shut my eyes for a second and sighed. "I'm tired. I need to rest."

Technically, I had paid my rent through the end of the month, so the room was mine. I went to my vacant room and fell asleep on the blue carpet. When I awoke several hours later, I tried to speak with my roommate, but he was adamant.

"Please, just leave."

The other council members had coerced him to shun me. Why the ongoing hatred? What had I done to invoke such anger?

That evening I packed my car and went to a nearby motel. I tried to get along the best I could financially, looking to God for a thread of strength. Somehow, I managed.

———— ◆◆ ————

Without Cornerstone, I needed to focus my heart on anything other than Cornerstone, so I became heavily involved with *The Promise*, which began rehearsals for its fifth season in mid-April. During that time, I hung out with friends in Glen Rose: the president of Promise Productions, Dr. Ron Corley, his wife, Karan, and Boo and Robert Summers.

Robert is a renowned, all-American artist, painter, and sculptor, most notably known for his larger-than-life bronze display, "The Cattle Drive," featured in downtown Dallas's western glory. With its three bronze cowboys on horseback driving forty-nine cattle, it's considered the largest bronze sculpture in the world. Robert is an absolute genius in his field. Most important to me is that Robert is a born-again believer.

Because of the daily performances, Boo invited me to stay with her and Robert in Glen Rose. Besides, I needed the distance from the Cornerstone nightmare.

The Summers lived in what appeared to be the smallest house in an upper-middle-class neighborhood, but it was an illusion. I spotted their one-story home at the end of the block, noting its massive roof.

Boo and a house filled with radiant light welcomed me at the door. I gawked at the fifteen-foot wide circular skylight overhead: A stained-glass mosaic of white doves flying in circles through blue skies and clouds, designed by Boo and handcrafted by Robert. When the sun hit, it created a spectacular heavenly natural light display.

To the left of the entry, a winding staircase curved below. To the right, an elevator waited as alternative transportation to the other floors below. In front of me was a massive glass wall that opened into a breathtaking view of rolling hills and trees for miles. I realized their home sits on the side of a cliff, and we were standing on the top, the fourth floor.

A few hundred feet out, I could see miles of rolling green hills with a white building surrounded by a sea of evergreen trees that doubled as Robert's studio and an observatory, complete with music, paintings, sculptures, and bagpipes—the ultimate man-cave.

As we descended the stairs, Boo gave me a tour. The fourth floor was the entrance and lobby to the home. The bedrooms and bathrooms were on the third floor. The kitchen, dining room, and offices were on the second floor. The first floor hosted their living room and the den, where Robert's custom-built furniture filled the room. Between Robert and Boo, they have created a magnificent masterpiece of a home.

During my stay, we ate dinner together and talked about the arts and the things of God. With all the recent pain and drama from my situation with Cornerstone, being with this sweet couple was a balm to my soul. I could have stayed forever, but God had other plans for me.

The Promise opened a five-month run of performances in June with shows every weekend until October. My salary from the performances was enough for me to live on.

A month into our shows, I heard from a friend in Dallas that Cornerstone had just closed its doors and was no longer in production. *What?* My heart sank as I considered the disaster the council had caused. Cornerstone was my baby, and I needed to go back to Irving to see what they had done to her. A cloud of sadness followed me as I drove.

When I got to the theatre, the door was ajar, the building abandoned. Everything I had worked for and the money I had spent on costumes, props, lights, and the sound was gone. The computers, phones, desks, chairs, and fax machines were gone from the office. The council had taken it all.

I made a few phone calls and learned that the theatre failed due to the lack of interest from the public. I felt something like this would happen, but I was surprised that it only took six months to crumble.

At that moment, I realized that God anoints whom He calls, and there can be no substitute. I was God's anointed, called to start this ministry, chosen, and empowered by the Holy Spirit. Not because of my talent or skill but because the Lord put me in that position and mandated me to spearhead that dream into a unique theatre ministry. But it had been hijacked, and God had a few things to say about His stolen property.

The council thought they could run Cornerstone better than I, so they voted me out. And when it failed, the new staff kicked it to the curb, deserted, left in tatters, and drowning in $40,000 worth of debt. Would they pay for their damages? Not hardly.

I spoke to a lawyer friend. He told me that I could have them arrested for all they had done, but I didn't feel right going that route.

> *But instead, one brother takes another to court—and this*
> *in front of unbelievers! The very fact that you have lawsuits*
> *among you means you have been completely defeated already.*
> *Why not rather be wronged? Why not rather be cheated?*
> *—1 Corinthians 6:6–7*

The council left a huge debt and a legal mess for me to clean up. But it was my baby, my heart, my dream, and even though I didn't cause Cornerstone's demise, I nonetheless felt responsible. So I chose to be cheated rather than bring shame to God's kingdom.

One of the council members took me to a storage unit where they had stored some of the items, but with no theatre to use them nor funds to pay for the storage, I declined.

I went back to work to pay off the debt. I found a job as a credit analyst for a credit firm during the week while performing with *The Promise* on weekends. Even though I got paid well, I put all my earnings towards Cornerstone's creditors and clients and lived on the small salary *The Promise* paid me.

I felt as if I had no purpose in my life anymore. I felt like a failure, merely existing. Cornerstone had been my mission. My only mission now was to pay back the debt.

Spiritually, I yearned to follow the Lord, but the devil had a field day in my mind.

"You're a failure!" I heard the devil taunt me. *"Everyone thinks you're sinning. So you might as well go back to the way you were and sin."*

As tempting as it was, I couldn't do that to God or myself. Instead, I prayed.

"Lord, thank You for giving me a chance to serve You. I know I've let You down, but I pray someday You'll trust me again and allow me to do something great for You and Your kingdom."

I felt a faint glimmer of hope nudge my heart.

I lift up my eyes to the mountains—where does my help come from? My help comes from the Lord the Maker of heaven and earth.

—Psalm 121:1–2

With my newfound love for everything Russian, I was more than delighted to run across some new students from eastern Europe who were attending my alma mater, Christ for the Nations. Vladimir and Elena, a beautiful young couple from Russia, quickly became friends. Knowing I was excited about their native home, Elena was thrilled to indulge me. They shared Russian meals with me and their language, music, culture, and stories from their homeland. I couldn't have been happier.

I also met from Ukraine: Valentin and Tatiana from Odessa, Valeriy from Kyiv, and three teenage young men from Moldova, Victor, Alexander, and Vali.

Since the destruction of my ministry and betrayal by my church, I felt a bit of a pariah. With these eight new souls from the post-Soviet Union, I found a new family I loved being with, and the feeling was mutual.

My new friends introduced me to different perspectives on the world. When Elena first entered an American grocery store, she told me she gasped at all the produce. Never had she seen such abundance in Russia.

When Elena's mother, Nadia, visited from Russia, I invited her to join me on an errand one hot day. While we were out, I asked, "Would you like some ice cream?"

She responded in her beautiful Russian language with a nod, "*Da*" (yes).

She expected us to go home and have some. Her eyes grew large when I pulled into an ice cream shop's drive-thru window, ordered two double-dipped cones, drove to the window, paid, got our order, and continued on our way.

A childlike grin below her wide eyes spread across her face. Taking her cone, she asked, "How did you do that?"

"Oh, that?" I pointed with my cone to the shop. I tried to explain in my fractured Russian, "There are a lot of drive-up food restaurants here in America. Someday, maybe Russia will have them too."

For the longest time, she licked her cone in silence. Finally, she said, "America…" and nodded her approval. "For the people." And she saluted me with her cone.

I smiled and saluted her back. "America!"

I prayed for the freedom we take for granted here in America to spread to the former Soviet Union. I realized then that in many countries worldwide, people's lives are made harder by political oppression. Americans strive to make life easier for each other—that's capitalism. Our freedom can only be appreciated by leaving the USA and living for a while in socialist countries.

———◆◆———

On the weekends, I introduced my adopted sons—Victor, Vali, and Alexander (Sasha)—to American culture and places of interest. When I asked to take a picture of them, they stood like solemn smileless statues.

"Hey, Sasha," I joked, "tell Victor and Vali to smile, would you? And, by the way, you can smile too."

They broke their solemn faces long enough to explain. "In eastern Europe, to smile without reason shows you are not intelligent. It looks foolish."

Foolish? That caught me off guard. It took some convincing, but I finally got them to loosen up enough to smile for a picture.

I realized that Victor was incredibly embarrassed to smile. In Moldova, most of his teeth had been pulled and replaced with gold ones. In communist countries, you have free social medicine, but smiles come with unsightly gold instead of matching porcelain. I made an appointment with a dentist in Dallas. Within a week, Victor sported a beautiful white smile.

Valeriy from Ukraine was closer to my age and an intellectual, so our conversations were mostly about what fascinated us most: The Bible and theology. In our discussion, he said, "The only Bible available to read in eastern Europe is the old Orthodox Russian version, which no one reads." He settled back in his chair; his brows pinched, and his eyes shifted in thought. "Richard, I believe my mission in life will be to translate the entire Bible from Hebrew, Aramaic, and Greek into modern Russian."

Valeriy's endeavor was incredibly bold, but I wasn't sure if he realized what a mammoth project he would be undertaking, although his motives were pure.

We prayed to the Lord and asked for this undertaking to be blessed. And can you believe it? For the next twenty years, Valeriy would do precisely that. By 2015 he had not only translated the Bible into Russian, but he started over and translated it into the Ukrainian language too.

Valeriy turned out to be an undeniable powerhouse for the Lord in Ukraine—a mighty warrior wielding God's words on paper so his kinsmen could understand the promise of life held within those pages. Today, he's the toast of Bible societies in Ukraine and a speaker on deep theological topics.

Mighty, yes. But like Sampson, I found his weakness: Braum's ice cream! Valeriy had never had a banana split before, so he was in heaven after one bite. After that, many theology discussions and Bible studies took place over banana splits. I never knew devotions could be so tasty… and fattening.

———◆••◆———

In 1994, we held auditions for *The Promise's* seventh season. Then I heard the good news: The Promise received an invitation to perform at the Kremlin State Palace in Moscow for the second year in a row. *Yes!* This time it would only be a five-day run starting in November, right after our scheduled performances in Glen Rose ended. I wrote my friends, Dima and Ilya, in Moscow that I would be coming back, and they were as delighted as I was.

During this time, I continued to work by day at the credit firm, paying off Cornerstone's bills and trying to raise money for my next trip to Russia. Our show in Glen Rose finally ended in October, and we were off to Moscow. I could hardly wait.

The day after arriving in Moscow, I met up with Dima and Ilya at the rehearsals. While they both worked as light technicians for the Kremlin theatre, I acted on stage in the same role I had been doing in Glen Rose. We were ready, and we opened to packed houses each night through the end of November. God once again worked through us and in the hearts of the Russian people. Many came to know Jesus as their Lord and Savior.

It was such a blessing to meet so many people in Moscow. But more exciting than that, pastors invited me to visit their churches. Would I be back? You bet I would.

Our five-show run had just ended. It was time to leave Russia, but I wanted to spend more time with Dima before leaving. His family had given their hearts to Jesus when we met in 1993, and I wanted to see how they were all doing in their faith. They were attending a church!

On the plane, I had time to reflect. Russia turned out to be a respite from all the hurt I experienced with Cornerstone. I looked out the window with renewed hope in my heart, but the tears were gone this time. I smiled.

HEALING
BEGINS

Since the betrayal at Cornerstone, I had been battling depression. My former assistant pastor's breach of confidentiality left me emotionally confused, and I didn't feel safe attending that church. I had to find a new church to call home.

One of the actors from *The Promise* told me about a church in Carrollton and invited me to meet him there. I recalled that this was one of the churches we ministered at when I sang with Living Praise a decade earlier. After the service, the pastor approached me.

"I know you!" He pointed a finger. "You're the director of Cornerstone."

I wasn't quite sure how to react. Had the pastor heard about the fallout? Would he judge me from what he heard? Would I be embraced or shunned? I did the only thing that came naturally to me—I blushed. I was relieved to learn that he knew nothing of what had happened.

"My wife and I came to see your shows for the last few years. You did a nice, professional job. Our church members love your ministry."

I don't think I'll ever get tired of hearing positive responses like that about my shows. It's nice to know that I was making a difference.

That day I joined the church. The new year brought new hope, new friends, and a change within me.

The church was in the midst of an enormous building project. Before long, they were ready to move into their new building, and the church was looking for artists to paint the children's rooms—finally, something I could lend my gifts and hands to.

Keeping busy with this new building project was a godsend—I felt needed once again, and even more important, I felt wanted. Cornerstone, the theatre, was no longer around. But the Lord gave me an epiphany: I was Cornerstone. Cornerstone was in me, and wherever I went, there would be a Cornerstone production. Thank You, Lord!

> *The stone which the builders rejected has become the cornerstone.*
>
> —Psalm 118:22

The trips to Russia in 1993 and '94 confirmed within me a love for eastern Europe and its people. Promise Productions would not be returning in 1995, but I couldn't get the Russian people out of my heart. I prayed earnestly that the Lord would open opportunities. That's when I felt the Lord speak to me, "*Take a group yourself.*"

What? Me?

We could go if I could find someone capable of organizing and leading a ministry troupe back to Russia. I believed the lie from the

Cornerstone council that I was not a good leader. So I told fellow Promise cast members about this new theatre ministry we would call CornerstoneArts. I knew plenty of people who had been with me in Russia who would love to go back. After a while, I had gathered a group of interested actors. Now, if I could only find a leader to head such an expedition, we'd be all set.

One invitation after another affirmed my dream of returning to Russia.

- Dan, a former CFNI student and friend, was now a missionary in St. Petersburg. He invited our group.
- Valeriy, my Ukrainian friend from CFNI, was back in Kyiv, and he extended an invitation.
- Victor, my Moldovan friend from CFNI, invited our group to come and minister.

I now had three invitations in Europe even before we were ready to leave the USA.

Over the next few months, while waiting for a director to emerge, I organized the group. I wrote a drama and choreographed dances, especially for our tour.

My leadership skills were substantiated in other, sometimes unusual, and confusing ways. One day, I was called into the vice president's office at the finance firm where I was still working.

"You are a great worker, Richard," she began. I felt my ego rise. "Your work output is prompt, and your quality is consistently high." She paused, studying me while choosing her words carefully. "I hope you'll understand what I'm about to say."

My ego turned to curiosity. It sounded like she was about to give me a promotion with a raise. I had visions of paying off Cornerstone's debt faster.

"You're fired."

What? I was fired? I was speechless. She went on.

"You can fight this if you want, and you will win, and we would gladly take you back. But Richard, I want to ask you something. Why are you here? This job is not where you're supposed to be. You're tremendously talented in the arts, yet you're hiding here in a cubicle. Why?"

She leaned forward and looked me in the eye. "You're a leader, Richard…"

Did she just say leader?

"…and you need to find your place, and this job isn't it. You're a leader. I also have a word for you: go where you're celebrated, not just tolerated."

She was exactly right. I was hiding here. Hiding from ministry. I had been hurt, and although I was bored here, it was safe. I needed to get back into ministry. I packed up my desk, said goodbye to my coworkers, and drove home, disappointed and excited at the same time.

Lord, what are You doing?

———————— ✦ ————————

The Promise's theatre season closed at the end of October 1995. A leader had not yet emerged from our new theatre group to Russia. And now, my former boss's words reverberated in my mind.

You're a leader.

I tried to shake those words. It's amazing how God can corner you into His will. I knew what I must do. Reluctantly, I volunteered.

Our team was thrilled with my decision, and that gave me confidence. I had already been making all the technical arrangements to get us back to Russia: housing, transportation, ministry locations, assistants, translators, etc. Finally, the day came; we boarded a plane and were off to Moscow.

Our ministry would consist of short skits and choreography to Western songs and patriotic American numbers—all the things that Russians were fascinated with about our culture. We wrapped up with the gospel drama, a message, and an invitation to receive Jesus as Lord.

Yulia, a Russian friend from my last trip to Moscow, was our interpreter and met us at the airport. The next day, we arrived in Moscow and had rehearsals. We then boarded a train to St. Petersburg to minister first at Pastor Dan's church.

Vica, a twenty-year-old Russian girl, was my assistant. As she led me to buy some supplies, we had to stop for her to rest. I sat beside her.

"Hey, Vica, are you okay?" I said in my broken Russian.

"My feet." She pulled a foot out of her worn slip-on Naugahyde shoe and wiggled her toes. "It's my shoes. They hurt me."

I asked the obvious American question, "Why don't you wear a more comfortable pair?"

Vica blushed and looked away. "I do not have another pair. Maybe someday."

I also blushed. I gathered my thoughts. How quickly I'd forgotten the economic circumstances of most Russians. For most, two pairs of shoes would have been a luxury.

"Hey, Vica." I nudged her gently with my shoulder. "Is it okay if I bless you with a new pair of shoes?"

Her eyes met mine for a moment to see if I was serious.

"Oh no, Richard. I was not suggesting such a thing. It will take just a moment, and I will be fine."

We continued walking, resting, and talking more while I persisted with my offer to buy her new shoes. Eventually, Vica allowed me to bless her, not with just one set of shoes but with two—one for everyday comfortable walking and one for special occasions.

Later, my friend Dan confided in me that Vica told him that my gesture of kindness changed her life and how she felt about herself. It's incredible how such a small gift can change a person's life.

> *It is more blessed to give than to receive.*
>
> —Acts 20:35

With our St. Pete tour nearing an end, snow was falling when we arrived back in Moscow at the end of November. We hosted a huge meal for both Americans and Russians together. It was also our last farewell to a successful missionary group.

While most of the team returned to the States, I remained behind with two team members, Mark and Brian. I had personal invitations to reconnect with my friends Valeriy in Ukraine and Victor in Moldova.

Months before we left, I had instructed both Mark and Brian to order their Ukrainian visas. Mark had his visa, but Brian wanted to save money and chose the unethical way of bribing the border officials with $20.

He insisted, "It's easier than getting a visa." I didn't appreciate the risk he was taking or the shady nature of his approach, but it was too late now. He was on his own.

"Your passports, please." The border official held out a gloved hand.

Mark and I presented our passports, and with a quick verification, the official stamped our passports and handed them back. However,

Brian shrugged to the officer and slid a twenty-dollar bill inconspicuously into his passport with a sly smile.

"I'm sorry, officer, I didn't have time to buy a passport. I was hoping you could help me, is that okay?"

There was a moment of awkward silence in the standoff. The border official's face turned serious while Brian's smile looked less authentic as the $20 dangled like a carrot. Without much emotion, the official took the twenty.

"Have a seat," and he walked on.

Brian's smile widened as we locked eyes. "See, I told you it would work."

He had illegally bought his way through this border crossing. He didn't have a stamp in his passport, but that didn't bother him. It did me.

We arrived in Kyiv and met Valeriy at the train station. It was good to see him again and see the humble beginnings of his Bible translations into the Ukrainian language. He escorted us to his flat in downtown Kyiv.

"Richard, I've finished the New Testament." His eyes got big. "I must show you. Come."

He led me to his den, where a mountain of books in the Greek and Hebrew languages were opened to different pages around a stack of papers typed neatly in Ukrainian.

"I have finished my first edition. Look. After it is typeset properly, I will have it printed. My people will be able to read God's story in their own language." He looked up. "It is good, Richard. Very good."

Over the past twenty-five years since then, Valeriy has translated the entire Ukrainian Bible and created a linear Russian/Ukrainian interpretation. He has become a noted author of Bible translations in Ukraine and has enjoyed success and awards for his lifelong achievements.

During my time in Kyiv, Valeriy introduced me to a bright and zealous young pastor from Nigeria. He invited me to do a show at his church the following year. How wonderful to have churches already giving me invitations to come and minister. I would come back for the next few years and minister at his church with much success. With his infectious personality and fiery sermons, his church membership grew into the tens of thousands.

Sadly, like so many who skyrocket into stardom, he came crashing down from extramarital affairs and financial scandals. After fines, threats of being deported, and a short stint in jail, he was back trying to start a new church, but with his questionable past, few now attend his congregation. I, too, declined further invitations to do shows with him.

Valeriy showed us around Kyiv, and we had a wonderful sojourn under his hospitality. It was time to follow our tight schedule. We hugged Valeriy, said our goodbyes, and then boarded the train to Moldova.

We had entered Ukraine without incident, but now we needed to exit and go through passport control again on the train. A senior Ukrainian border official was training a team of three new border guards. Mark and I dutifully presented our passports and visas and were good to go. Brian, however, feigned ignorance again and tried slipping the official a $20 note in his passport.

The border officer took one look at the money offered, turned to the three in training, and motioned them closer. Big mistake. Wrong timing and wrong man. Holding up the $20 bill, I knew enough of the Ukrainian language to hear what was going on.

"See the American bribe this traveler is offering me? At times, you will find a foreigner who comes to visit our country without bothering to get a visa. They think they are clever and do not need to abide by our country's laws. If visitors do not see the need to follow the simplest of our travel protocols, they are likely to break more of our laws. When you see this happen, you must escort them off the train at the next train stop and have them arrested."

He turned to Brian and said in broken English, "Take your bribe. Do not leave seat until Transnistria. You leave train. Next time you visit our country, you obey laws."

Brian's face turned beet red. He pocketed the twenty and sat down.

I knew this would happen. The officer made an example of Brian in front of the young border guards and kicked him off the train at the next stop. At least they were not going to arrest him.

Brian looked at me as if I could somehow fix his premeditated blunder and make it go away.

I couldn't believe it. How irresponsible and insulting as a traveling guest in a foreign country. This train ride and his schedule were derailed.

When we reached the small breakaway state of Transnistria, in the middle of a snowstorm, two of the border trainees escorted Brian from the train. I couldn't get off with him, as I must meet Victor and other pastors in the morning, but Mark volunteered to stay behind with him. I gave Mark Valeriy's phone number and told him to contact him to pick them up, and I would try to reunite with them in a few days.

Victor greeted me when I arrived in Moldova the following day. I told him what happened to one of my companions with the border patrol and the other staying behind with him. I hoped they would be fine until we could reconnect.

Over the next few days, I enjoyed a good conversation with Victor and his father, an important bishop over Pentecostal churches in Moldova. We discussed the possibility of our troupe performing a show at their church.

Moldova is a poor country, and Victor's home had no indoor plumbing, only an outhouse behind his home. One night I needed to use it at 3 a.m. In January. In four feet of snow. With freezing winds whipping all around. It was an unwelcome wake-up call. Afterward, I tried to stand, but I couldn't. I was stuck to the seat! It took some well-placed spittle to free me. Oh, the sheer indignity of it all! I don't know if I was red from the cold or from embarrassment. After that, I learned not to eat or drink anything after 6 p.m.

Victor was dating a wonderful young lady named Emilia, whom he would later marry. I accompanied him to visit her as a chaperone. Their culture doesn't allow him into her family's home, as it's considered impolite for a single man to see a single woman in her home. So he courted her just outside her door while I gave them some distance for some privacy, trying not to freeze. Victor was too in love to realize he was cold.

After a few days with Victor and meeting church leaders about a possible production the following year, I caught a train back to Kyiv. I had no idea where to find Mark and Brian. So I contacted Valeriy. To my relief, Valeriy had contacted Mark by cell phone. Because Mark had his documents, he took a train back to Ukraine. But because Brian didn't have the proper papers, he wasn't allowed on any public transportation crossing the border, so he had to walk several miles in knee-deep snow across barren snowy fields far from the Transnistrian border patrol stations to get back into Ukraine. Valeriy found Brian muddy, wet, and freezing. He drove him back to Kyiv and housed him there until I returned.

When I met up with Brian at Valeriy's flat, he was mad at me. He thought I should have gotten off the train to stay with him. But I had scheduled appointments to keep, meeting obligations, and ministry invitations to secure. I quickly reminded him I had insisted he get his Ukrainian documents in order before we left for our Russian tour. I did not see it as my role or responsibility to comfort a huckster caught manipulating Ukrainian law. It was a challenging and humbling lesson for him and a tough-love aspect of my leadership.

Uzhgorod, Ukraine

FUSION OF CHURCH AND THEATRE

In 1996, my home church moved into its new building. Over the months, I painted children's rooms when the pastor came by one hot August morning.

"Hey, Richard, looks great. Nice job." He moved around the room with his hands behind his back, observing the details and theme of the artwork. "You know we're looking to build our arts program. You think you'd like to head up the department?"

I almost dropped my paintbrush.

"Pastor! I'm blessed doing this and would like to do more to serve the church. I'd be honored to take over the department."

So I created the art department the following month. That fall, I put together our first theatrical production. I then propelled that momentum into another more powerful drama, *The Judgment Seat*, by my friend Russ Houck—a story about people who have died and find themselves standing before the Lord to give an account for their lives. It's a wonderfully powerful, funny, but profound way to urge people to prepare themselves for eternity. We opened the production at the church. I invited Russ and his beautiful wife, Brenda, to join us. It was a great honor to have them in the audience on opening night for our church's presentation in Dallas.

My pastor remembered firsthand the potential of theatre ministry when he and his church attended Cornerstone's productions, and now he wanted this same impact for his growing church. Directing these shows brought healing to my raw soul and emotions. I felt vindicated and worthy to once again be used for God's kingdom. The two worlds of theatre and reality I had desired my whole life were, for the first time merging into one world.

------- ◆◆ -------

A church member and travel agent, Leah Deslauriers, invited me to join a group of pastors on an all-expense-paid trip to the Holy Land.

Honored and excited but baffled, I asked her why she'd chosen me.

"I think you deserve it, Richard," is all she'd say.

We arrived in Tel Aviv fifteen hours later, met the other pastors in our group, and boarded our tour bus for the last leg to our hotel.

In Israel, I loved seeing the sights I had so often read about in the Bible. It was almost surreal knowing that Jesus had walked the same road I was walking, taught on the temple steps where I was standing, prayed at Gethsemane, been crucified on Golgotha, and then rose again from the tomb that we had just explored. What an incredible cultural, historical, and spiritual experience. No wonder I was constantly blinking back tears.

Years ago, I had directed a theatrical production based on the best-selling book *The Hiding Place*, the true story of the life of Corrie ten Boom, a Dutch Christian woman who hid Jews fleeing from the Nazis during World War II. She was betrayed and sent to a concentration camp. So I was particularly interested in learning more about this horrific period for the Jews.

Leah took us to Yad Vashem, a sobering yet beautiful memorial and museum dedicated to those who perished in the Holocaust. Outside the museum, the Avenue of the Righteous, one can find a garden area of hundreds of trees planted in long rows along both sides of the street. Leah explained the significance of the trees. Each tree was planted in honor of those who went beyond the call of duty to help the Jewish people. Then she focused on the smallest of trees—planted in honor of Corrie ten Boom.

Originally Corrie's tree was as tall as all the others when they were planted and dedicated on May 1, 1962. But something supernatural happened on the day Corrie died in 1983. A lightning storm over Jerusalem struck her tree, causing it to die on the same day she did. Shortly thereafter, they replanted a new tree in its place. It stands out smaller than the other trees as if to bring attention specifically to Corrie and her life.

Leah then pointed to me in front of everyone.

"Because of Richard's work to bring to life this beautiful story through a theatrical production, this changed my life to begin a work to bring Jews and Christians together, and we all stand here because of him."

> "I will bless those who bless you, and whoever curses you I will curse, and all peoples on earth will be blessed through you."
>
> —Genesis 12:3

I was so surprised. I now understand why Leah offered me this trip to the Holy Land. She wanted to touch my life much like I suppose I touched her life. We rarely know what impact we're having on others through our work.

---◆●◆---

When I started to work for my church, I let my pastor know that my heart was in missions. He remembered and agreed that since summer is slow for churches, including ours, I could take those months to travel and do mission trips. So I did. I accepted an invitation from a pastor I had met the year before, who invited me to do a show for his church.

After landing in Moscow, I took a train to Kazan, Russia, prepared the local church actors, and opened a performance of *The Judgment Seat* to the public. After the show, I took a train to Kyiv, Ukraine, where I would meet up with my friend Valeriy and his Nigerian pastor.

In Kyiv, I was to put on my first of many shows. My Russian was still in the formative rough state, so I was assigned a lovely interpreter, Vitalina. With Vita's help, I held auditions. The show went beautifully, with many coming to know Christ for the first time. My cast was so excited about the show that they asked if they could continue performing it around Ukraine. Of course, that was fine with me, but I had an appointment with another church in Odessa and couldn't stay with them. So, before I left, I helped them form their own travel group and condensed a smaller, travel-sized set they could easily take to various churches. And for the next few years, this small yet mighty team of believers presented our play all around Ukraine, bringing thousands to the Lord. I was so proud of them.

In August, I took a train to Odessa, Ukraine, to organize and direct a show with friends from CFNI a decade earlier, Pastors Valentin and Tatiana, and their Bible students. The show went well, and I saw many responses to the Holy Spirit's touch on the public's hearts.

---◆●◆---

Returning to my church, I put together a new Christmas musical. I was busy with the church, and my future looked bright as we finished out the year.

In 1997, the season's schedule was almost identical to the previous year. I directed shows at my church and took more trips to eastern Europe in summer, expanding God's kingdom through theatrical productions.

One evening in Dallas, before a rehearsal with all my actors, we stood in a circle for prayer. Suddenly, something incredible happened. I had a supernatural vision. My body started to grow. I kept getting larger until my right foot stood on the East Coast of the United States, my left foot stood on the West Coast, and my head was in space looking down on the earth. The Lord spoke to me.

"What do you see?"

I looked around at the world and said, "I see Canada in front of me, Lord. Central and South America behind me, Europe and Africa to my right, and all of Asia to my left."

The voice declared, "Everywhere you can see is where I will take you."

As quick as that, I snapped out of the vision. The curious thing was that I was praying the whole time for the rehearsal while I had the vision. When I said, "Amen," none of the actors knew what I had just witnessed, but some wondered why I was staring at the floor with a look of astonishment on my face. Had the Lord just opened the entire world to me?

Someone spoke up, "Are you okay?"

I shook myself awake, "Oh. I was just thinking about something. Okay, everyone, turn in your scripts to scene four..."

———◆•◆———

That summer, I was off again with an invitation back to Russia and Kyiv to do *The Judgment Seat*. More auditions. More rehearsals. More performances. More souls!

Back in Dallas in the fall, I was preparing for a production. I wanted to work with the Spanish branch of our church. I felt they should participate in my shows, too, with a Spanish cast reaching the Spanish public.

I met the Spanish fine arts director, Viviana Andrade. She was a lovely young lady who loved to travel and loved the arts. I worked with Viviana to translate *The Judgment Seat* into Spanish and then direct the Spanish and English actors simultaneously. This would be the first translation of this drama into another language. The show has since been translated into eighteen languages.

It was an exciting opening night. For the first time ever, I would direct two shows in two different languages with two different casts at the same time. We started with the English production, then later that same evening, we opened the Spanish version. Both shows saw a tremendous harvest. It was such a blessing to work with my Spanish actors. But I especially loved working with Viviana, whose heart was like my own, to minister through the arts.

The new year, 1999, presented many opportunities to do shows. I wanted to introduce a new springtime musical at my church called *The Bride*. It's a romantic story of a love affair the Lord has for His church and how He guides her from a young child into maturity. With the success of our fall show in English and Spanish, I wanted to produce something more ambitious, this time a musical. I would work closely with Viviana on the Spanish production and cast her in the title role. She was the instrument God used to establish a Spanish drama ministry that would eventually take us to Mexico and beyond. The actors that were part of the productions at the Spanish church would continue to minister with me in Central and South America.

Sadly, Vivi passed away after just a few years of knowing and loving her. She lived a life that bore so much fruit in such a short time, and her work continues to bear fruit today.

———◆•◆———

Summer always means travel, and I had another invitation. This time I would take a group of dancers from my church in Dallas to help present *The Bride* in Ukraine with me. In June, I flew to Kyiv to prepare the Ukrainian actors, with my interpreter and friend Vita by my side. In July, it was time for the American dancers to arrive. What a blessing to have my artists from two different worlds unite for one project.

The show was a success, but the highlight of the trip was meeting Pastor Henry Madava of Victory Church. Over time, he would become a close friend.

As a result of the success of our show, pastors in Crimea invited me to come and work with them to produce *The Judgment Seat*.

———◆•◆———

In Yalta, Crimea, after weeks of rehearsals, I enjoyed a day off with my interpreter, Victor, who invited me to go to the Black Sea for an afternoon on the beach.

Sitting on the sand in my blue swim trunks, lazily watching the waves ebb in and out under a warm sun, Victor pointed across the waters.

"Richard, see that wall over there?"

I looked where he pointed and saw a stone wall jutting out into the sea just beyond a slimy green pier.

"Yes."

"On the other side of that is a small, remote island. It is beautiful. Do you want to swim to it?"

I assessed the situation and felt uneasy about venturing beyond the sand where I was sitting.

"I don't know, Vic. I'm not much of a swimmer. I can swim one, maybe two laps in a pool, and then I sink like a rock."

"It is not far, Richard. I know you can do it."

Despite my better judgment, I shrugged and agreed to swim to this pretty, tiny island of his… "just around the corner."

Vic stood and took off with me right behind him, kicking up sand. Splashing ahead of me, he dove into a wave and came out the other side like a professional swimmer with an impressive freestyle technique. He was around the wall and heading for the elusive island in no time.

I hopped and bobbed over the first wave, then took off into the ocean in an unimpressive freestyle, head above water. I swam about halfway to the end of the pier and realized that it was farther than I expected. I needed to rest.

I went to the stone wall to grab hold of something to catch my breath, but the slippery seaweed wouldn't let me grip the wall. I kept treading water and thinking about the situation. The obvious choice should have been to swim back to shore, but I was close to the end of the pier and this unseeable island, remembering what Victor said. It "was just on the other side of the wall." I decided to tough it out and go for it.

I struggled to the end of the pier. That's when I saw the island. It was way out there! It was nowhere near the pier, as I was told. Now what? Dread rushed over my tired body. I attempted again to rest on the wall, but I could not get a grip on it. I had no choice; I had to make it to the island.

"Relax and float," I told myself, but that wasn't working. I tried to dog paddle, float, backstroke, anything to keep my head above water in the middle of the Black Sea, but my arms and legs were cramping up. The pain was excruciating. I was slipping under the water. Dread turned to panic.

My situation was desperate.

There was no one nearby. I looked to the island and could see Victor lying casually on the beach, seemingly asleep. I tried to call out, but my voice was barely audible, as often happens when someone is drowning. I tried to relax again, but nothing seemed to help. My limbs betrayed me and stopped working. I sank below the rippling waters, struggling to reach the surface. I looked up, swallowing seawater, and saw the liquid border between life and death. I prayed a final plea, *"Lord, help me."*

I started to blackout.

The strangest thing happened just then. A sudden force came over me. Somehow, I shot out of the water like a rocket. Then I heard a voice shout.

"Swim!"

A surge of adrenaline hit me, and with everything I had, I did what I was told and swam, thrashing about. I don't know how I did it, but somehow, I managed to reach the island.

My stomach was in knots, and every muscle shook in convulsions. I was so sick that I threw up seawater, coughing and wheezing, my lungs raging as if on fire. I lay on the shore for the longest time in a fetal position, wondering what had just happened.

I peeked over to Victor through weary eyes and saw that he was comfortably asleep—unaware of my close brush with death or the pathetic, embarrassing state I was currently in. If my eyes could have burned holes, Vic would have been riddled with them.

I lay there sick until he eventually woke. He looked at me lying in the sand. Without a care in the world, he said, "Are you ready? Let's swim back."

I pushed myself to a shaking elbow and glared at him.

"Oh no!" I protested, shaking my sea-soaked head. "You swim back, and you get me a boat!"

It wasn't hard for him to determine that I meant what I said. Bewildered but afraid to ask for a reason, he slipped back into the water, swam to shore, and returned sometime later with a motor boat and its owner.

I was sick for the next two days, shaken by my near-death experience. Gathering my nerves, I reflected on what had happened. How was I able to reach the surface and swim to safety? I was drowning in the Black Sea. I can only surmise that the Lord must have sent an angel who pulled me back to the surface and commanded me to swim. I was out for the count, so this had to have been the only explanation. Strangely, I felt motivated about the whole situation. God had saved me. The Lord had something great in store for me and just proved it.

I adopted the phrase at this time, which has served me well over the years.

"The safest place you can ever be is in the center of God's will."

Back on my legs again, we did the show, and it was well-received. Yalta is a summer tourist destination due to the beauty of the mountains and the Black Sea. Every night, we had massive audiences from Ukraine, Russia, and other eastern European countries. Again, many people came to Jesus, so it was a fruitful run. However, had I drowned in the Black Sea a week before, this victory for the Lord would have never happened. He had planned this production so that many would come to Christ. He needed me to organize and direct this drama resulting in salvation for many. I attempted to do what was dangerous to me, but more importantly, my ministry. Therefore, God had to do something supernatural to save me.

Since then, I have vowed not to do anything that might jeopardize my life, health, or well-being, as the fusion of my church leadership position and ministry are vitally important to the Lord. This fusion results in the salvation of untold numbers of people worldwide now and in the future.

> *"So do not fear, for I am with you; do not be dismayed, for I am your God. I will strengthen you and help you; I will uphold you with my righteous right hand."*
>
> —Isaiah 41:10

NEW OPPORTUNITIES

Invitations come in a variety of ways, but mostly from pastors since they will host the show through their church. So I got a surprise invitation from one of my American actresses working as an English teacher in Poland. I had e-mailed her asking if she had confirmation from the pastor. Everything seemed alright, so I accepted the invitation.

When I arrived by train to Rzeszow, I was surprised to see two young men come in place of Betty. They explained that she had just quit her teaching job the day before and returned to America.

Quit? Why didn't she tell me?

Piotr and Marcin helped with my blue luggage and took me to the pastor. Pastor Marek was kind enough to visit with me. Betty hadn't told the pastor about me, our production, or her invitation! He knew nothing about why I was there.

"Well, I'm here for four weeks," I informed him. "With your approval, I can still arrange a fantastic theatrical show for your church and community." What I didn't say was that I had nowhere else to go, so I was praying he'd say yes.

I showed him a video of my shows, and he was impressed enough to consult his elders. They called a quick meeting, and all agreed—the show must go on, to my relief.

They took me to their guest housing, and then with the pastor's help, we cast the actors from his church and got ready to put on a successful show.

Most importantly, we shared the gospel with many Polish people. What looked like what might have been a disaster turned out fruitful for my ministry, their church, and the Polish people. In the following years, we would do many shows together, and Pastor Marek and his lovely wife, Eva, would become dear friends.

———— ◆◆ ————

Meanwhile, back home in Midland, Texas, God went to extraordinary lengths to get my younger brother's attention. I had been sharing the Lord with Ed for twenty-one years. I told him he needed to have a relationship with Jesus Christ. His response had always been the same. My brother and sister, Tony and Tina, had been born again many years earlier and were raising their families in church.

"Me and the man upstairs are like this…" Ed would hold his crossed fingers in front of me.

Well, that's not the same thing. Ed wasn't ready spiritually to see the truth and the expanse of the gospel. I continued to pray for him, but to be honest, I thought he was a lost cause. It frustrated me to hit this brick wall, but I didn't want to push him. Around the world, I see hundreds, thousands of people come to Christ, yet I couldn't seem to reach my own brother.

Jesus said to them, "A prophet is not without honor except in his own town, among his relatives, and in his own home."
—Mark 6:4

In October 1999, my sixteen-year-old niece, Melissa, Ed's daughter, found out that she had a tumor behind her right ear. She needed surgery to remove the cancerous mass and had a 50 percent chance of survival. Ed was so distraught that he looked to me for consolation. I tried my best to comfort him and suggested he could trust God. But, like usual, my brother didn't want to hear that. He interrupted me, "You know, Richard, I love Melissa so much. I would do anything for her. I would gladly take this cancer in her place. I would take the surgery in her place. I would even die in her place."

Ed didn't realize it, but he had just taken the words right out of our Savior's mouth. What an opportunity.

"Ed," I jumped in, "that's wonderful. Just like you said you'd die for Melissa, Jesus did exactly that in your place because He loves you."

Ed searched my face. Then he said something that surprised me so much that I didn't know at first how to respond.

"So what do I need to do to get saved?"

For a moment, I was speechless while I pondered his sincerity. I had talked to him about the Lord for twenty-one years, and he always brushed me off. Now, because of his daughter's dire situation, he wanted to know how to get saved?

I gathered my thoughts, and right there in the hospital, I had the sweetest moment leading Ed to the Lord.

"There is a time for everything and a season for every activity under heaven" (Ecclesiastes 3:1).

In this situation, God used Melissa's tumor to bring her father, my brother, to Jesus Christ. Not only is Ed my blood brother, but we are now spiritual brothers in Christ.

Melissa went through her surgery with no complications and today serves as a registered nurse, selflessly helping untold numbers of people.

A new year, a new decade, a new century, and a new millennium. And a surprising new chapter in my journeys.

Shortly after the beginning of 2000, my pastor called me into his office. His wife met me in his stead.

"Have a seat, Richard."

She adjusted herself in the chair while I settled into mine. Her fingers knitted together and rested on her lap.

"We love your shows, Richard. People still talk about them. What a blessing it's been. But we've come to a point where my husband's vision has changed about the fine arts department, and we need to go in a different direction. We're sorry, but we are closing the entire fine arts department."

And just like that, I was out of a job.

This development came out of the blue. I found some consolation in that the fine arts program was but one of several departments deemed unnecessary that needed to be canceled, so it wasn't just my staff and me.

I'd had enough experience with God closing one door to open another that I didn't panic. My faith was growing, maturing.

Another opportunity would come along, eventually. It was His doing, not the church. One of my favorite scriptures of peace swept over me.

> *Trust in the Lord with all your heart and lean not on your own understanding; in all your ways submit to him, and he will make your paths straight.*
>
> —Proverbs 3:5–6

After letting me go, the church decided to trash all the sets, costumes, and props. Thankfully, my friend Rick, the maintenance worker at the church, let me know.

"Hey, Richard, we have all your props and costumes here. They told us to throw them away, but it seems such a waste. Are you interested in them? If so, you gotta come and get them today."

I thanked him, then immediately rented a storage unit near the church, borrowed a truck, and went to work.

My fine arts department had grown to a staff of sixteen. Many of them, once laid off, left the church. I joined the church for different reasons—the Lord called me there. I wasn't about to leave because of money. God was my provision, not the church. And until the Lord moved me, this was home. I was curious to find out what the Lord had in store. It didn't take long to find out.

The following Sunday, a young, well-dressed couple approached me following the service. Marc and Kelly were new to the church, and Marc was an up-and-coming motivational speaker. He told me they were planning their first speaking engagement and needed someone to decorate the stage. He'd heard I was the guy to talk with about building scenery for his conference. We discussed the content of his message so I would know better how to decorate for his event. I realized that Marc's presentation was a show we could produce together.

We discussed each segment and theme to illustrate the points he would be teaching. Marc's heart and mine quickly bonded, and he gave me his blessing to move forward with creating sets, costumes, and props. The event would take place over three days, and he needed around twenty characters and twenty different theatrical sets and costumes to pull it off. The problem was and always seems to be finances.

Marc and Kelly were just getting started, so they couldn't afford to rent theatre pieces to make this idea fly. But I just so happened to have some freshly salvaged costumes and sets, courtesy of my church and lots of free time. We could do this!

With no budget, I volunteered my free time and delved into making the sets and creating costumes and props out of my garage. We would do our first event at the Adam's Mark Hotel ballroom in Dallas, Texas. The two students who had "rescued" me in Poland came to visit me. I recruited Piotr and Marcin to be my first crew for our brand-new event called *The View*.

We were all nervous about Friday night's opening show. Would anyone come? If they did, would they like it? They did come. And despite the chaos behind the curtain, *The View* premiered. We had fourteen sets ready to go, but we were still building another six sets while the show was in progress.

Saturday and Sunday, the curtains went up at 9 a.m., and the show went on till 10 p.m. But my crew and I worked from 6 a.m. to midnight building sets.

We were exhausted when it was all over, and we had loaded out. But we had a hit. Everyone loved Marc and the whole concept of the show. I, however, would need a week to recuperate.

————◆•◆————

Two dear friends from my church, Sean and Alison, were missionaries in Port Elizabeth, South Africa, working under Pastors Jimmy and Mariana Crompton. Sean and Alison told the pastors about my work, and they invited me to do a show at their church. This would be my first trip to South Africa, and I would be staying with the minister of music and her husband.

Entering their home, I noticed that the beds in their house were on cinder blocks. I asked my hosts, "Why?"

"Tokoloshi," came the answer.

"Excuse me?"

"We have trouble with Tokoloshi or pygmy demons. They're prevalent in this area among the Xhosa and Zulu people. They're small, but they cause problems at night, so raising the beds keeps them from jumping up on you when you're asleep."

Are they joking, or are they for real?

They seemed to be serious, but even so, as a born-again Christian, I stand on God's Word.

> *For the Spirit God gave us does not make us timid, but gives us power, love and self-discipline.*
>
> —2 Timothy 1:7

After dinner, I settled in for the evening in their guest bedroom, in a bed on cinder blocks. *Pygmy demons?* I mused as I drifted off to sleep.

During the night, I was awakened by the host's dog scratching at the door. I tried to ignore it, but the dog kept scratching and whimpering. *I must be sleeping in the dog's room, and I've locked it out.* I considered opening the door to let it in. *Once it's in its room,* I reasoned, *it'll go to sleep.*

I got up but reconsidered. *What if the dog wants to play, or it keeps making noise?*

I took a few steps towards the door, thought better of it, and went back to bed. I decided to ignore the scratching and finally fell back to sleep.

At breakfast, my hosts asked, "How did you sleep? Was the bed comfortable?"

"Yes, but your little dog kept me up. It kept scratching at the door."

The two looked at each other. "Umm… we don't have a dog."

A shiver crawled up my spine. *If that wasn't your dog, what in the world was it?*

Chapter 10: New Opportunities

The next night, I pulled the covers up to my chin and jumped at every little sound. The following night, I moved in with Sean and Alison, where thankfully, there were no demons.

After a day of auditions and rehearsals, I ventured out to see as much of South Africa's beauty as I could in my limited time. My most memorable event was at Seaview Game Park, where I got to play with lion cubs.

When we finally opened our show in Port Elizabeth, the locals loved it. The South African people are sensitive to the movement of the Holy Spirit, so we had a great harvest night after night.

Our show's run ended, and I prepared to return to the States. God and the pastor had other plans. Pastor Jimmy invited me to extend my stay and do a Christmas show with them.

Once again, the Lord had opened a door that I hadn't even seen. This invitation was especially a blessing because I had no plans for the rest of the year. Since I didn't have a script or music with me, I decided to write an original Christmas show. I titled it *A Christmas Spectacular*, and spectacular it was. Not only did I incorporate creative video footage to run throughout the show, but I also recruited several departments from the church to participate in dramas, skits, choir, and dance routines.

We rented the city's prestigious Opera House, with its chandeliers, red velvet seats, and wrought-iron balconies. It first opened in 1892 and was proclaimed a national monument in 1980 and is the only authentic Victorian theatre in Africa. We had a great run, and the audiences loved the show, which ended with a beautiful and inspirational Christmas nativity scene featuring the greatest gift ever given to man, Jesus Christ. I would do several more shows in the years to come in this marvelous venue.

All good things must come to an end, and though I still didn't know what the next year would hold for me, it was time for me to move on. I said goodbye, boarded my plane, and flew back to the USA.

Back home, I learned from fellow actors that a creative couple, Ed and Malona, had opened a Christian theatre company in north Dallas— Christian Arts Theatre Zone (CATZ). They knew of me from my work with Cornerstone a decade earlier and wanted to meet me. Soon they were allowing me to direct some shows in their new facility.

I already had my repertoire from Cornerstone, so this allowed me to let Ed and Malona choose which shows they wanted from my repertoire and wanted me to bring some new ideas to their theatre. Our relationship worked well, and I appreciated their confidence allowing me to direct my own productions. My shows attracted large audiences since many knew me from Cornerstone or from the theatrical productions I had done at my church. The public responded positively and financially. I was happy and was having a wonderful time. This schedule also allowed me to have the freedom to continue to travel.

I was surprised to hear back from Marc and Kelly. After the gigantic show we had created, I thought he'd never want to go that route again. I was wrong. The show went well enough the year before to warrant another show this year.

Marc and I share a passion for using drama to deliver a message. My shows deliver the gospel, whereas his shows deliver a motivational message. I remembered that in one weekend, the show ran for twenty-eight hours and included twenty-two different characters who needed costumes and props along with sets, so I prepared myself psychologically. Marc and I are crazy enough to love what we do. Our working relationship is a marriage made in heaven, although it feels like hell at the time of production. Again, I started creating, designing, and building sets with a minimal budget.

Marc was excited to have found a perfect place for this year's production and couldn't wait to tell me about it. In a sweet twist of irony, we would be presenting *The View* at... my old Cornerstone Theatre building! We had cranked out quality shows from my theatre in this venue just a decade earlier. The Lord graciously allowed me to come back for a major production one last time. Audiences filled the hall three days in a row. It was like in the old days. The work was exhausting, but the joy of being in my old theatre, with full houses each night, and working with artistic hearts like the Accetta's was all worth it. The Lord had graciously orchestrated all of this in a way that brought official closure to my Dallas ministry but in a positive, fulfilling way.

London, England

LEARNING TO WALK... BY FAITH

I teach about faith using an illustration: faith is like automatic doors; they're closed until you walk up to them when suddenly, *whoosh*, they open.

When I started Cornerstone, I remember starting a letter to my friends asking for financial support. In midsentence, the Lord confronted me.

"What are you doing? Haven't I called you into this ministry? I have called you, and I will provide for you."

"Lord," I retorted, "can I at least let them know some of my needs?"

The Lord responded, "If you believe I answer prayer, then you pray to Me. I'll talk to others, and they'll give to you accordingly."

Reluctantly, I accepted. I was not too fond of the Lord's proposition. I had to do some soul searching.

Since 1987, God has met all my "...needs according to His riches in glory by Christ Jesus" (Philippians 4:19).

To this day, I don't solicit financial help. I trust the Lord. If a church gives to my ministry, great. If they don't, that's fine with me too. I do this as a passion—a service to the Lord and His people. But I never ask for or expect anything in return.

My board members chide me, "You're a terrible businessman."

I reply with a wink, "Well, it's a good thing I'm not a businessman but a missionary."

When reviewing Cornerstone's financial reports, they must admit that the Lord always provides in surprising, remarkable ways.

———◆◆———

I had spent the spring and summer of 2002 doing shows with CATZ and with *The View* in Dallas, and then I found myself back in South Africa again in the fall, preparing for yet another show. During that time, I received a request from a pastor in Warsaw, Poland, to produce and direct a show there. God showed me the illustration of the automatic doors, which looked closed at the time, but He also reminded me they would not open unless I walked toward them. It was time to test my faith. I would need around $2500. I only had $120 to my name.

I closed my eyes and exhaled a prayer, "I'll try." I put legs to that trust, and I leaned on God to provide by faith.

My first step was to contact the church in Warsaw and confirm that I would arrive in six weeks and produce a show. They were delighted, but I was scared to death. That's when God doubled down on my floundering faith.

"Give away $100," I heard Him say.

"What, Lord? Isn't that going in the opposite direction of what I need to do?"

"Yes, Richard, it is. Now give the $100 to someone who's in need."

"But Lord, it's almost all I have. Are You sure?"

"It is My way. Have faith."

So I did and chose a couple I saw every Sunday at church. I gave, and it hurt—a lot. But then, I saw how my simple gift touched this poor elderly couple. It turned out that they had been trusting the Lord for funds to eat.

Their need was great; the giving was sweet, and the Lord was happy. So was I, for that matter. But now, all I had was twenty dollars and a six-week clock ticking before my scheduled trip to Poland.

The following week I learned that receiving a gift can take as much faith as giving one. A young family I met in South Africa had a two-year-old daughter with muscular dystrophy. Her mom tried to get her to stand daily, as it helps slow the muscle deterioration, but it was painful for the little girl, and she'd cry. It was heartbreaking to watch.

The parents had to take her to the hospital for expensive medical treatments. Despite their physical and financial trials, they offered me a gift of $500. Like me giving $100, they were obedient to trust God. I froze, eyeing the cash. It wasn't right for me to take what they so desperately needed. I was about to hand the gift back, but I felt the Lord warning me not to steal their blessing.

It was hard to receive their gift. So, with great thanks and prayer over their daughter, I accepted their gift. I had never expected it to hurt as much to receive a gift as it had to give one.

We all struggle at times with faith that stretches us. But I am constantly reminded of God's promises and provisions and cling to these comforting words of Jesus.

> *"Look at the birds of the air; they do not sow or reap or store away in barns, and yet your heavenly Father feeds them. Are you not much more valuable than they? Can any one of you, by worrying add a single hour to your life?"*
> —Matthew 6:26–27

Anna Traverse, a fun-filled, seventy-something-year-old, was a crowd favorite in our Dallas church's productions years ago and had become one of my dear friends. The public loved her performances in my shows, and now, Anna had become a star at church with an infectious bubbly personality and a zeal for life. She was one of those people you just loved hanging around.

I had seen her health slowly decline. I prayed over her and went overseas to South Africa to put on theatrical productions. The weeks quickly flew by as we prepared for our musical.

After our show ended in South Africa, I returned to Dallas to see Anna but heard that she had passed on to heaven. I went by her family's home to offer my condolences. As we spoke, they gave me a program from her funeral. I smiled as I read her obituary and gasped when I read the directive about memorials.

"Anna would like all gifts donated to Richard Montez's ministry."

The following week, $800 worth of gifts came to my mailbox. I now had $1,300, enough to buy my airline ticket to Poland—one week before the flight.

Thank you, Anna, for thinking of me.

Although I now had enough for my plane ticket, how was I to cover my expenses in Poland?

I called Lufthansa to reserve my flight. They put me on hold for so long that I almost hung up and called another airline. But I felt the Lord encouraging me to be patient, so I paced the floor and stayed on the phone waiting. Finally, the agent came back on.

"I'm sorry to keep you waiting so long, Mr. Montez. But I noticed that you had flown several times before with us. We have a new program called Miles and More. I took the time to calculate and found that you have enough air miles for a free flight. If you can hold on for just a bit more, I'll transfer you to that department."

A free flight?

I couldn't believe it. God was showing off now, and it was blowing my mind.

I now had a free flight and $1300 in hand for my duration in Poland. God indeed provided, just like He promised.

In a sweet ending to this story of God's provision, the hospital in South Africa had started an experimental medical regimen for its muscular dystrophy patients. The young couple who trusted God and gave me the $500 gift found out that their daughter was eligible to be enrolled in this experimental treatment at no charge. She was healed and can now run like all the other children. God had also rewarded them for their obedience! Indeed, God's ways are so much better!

After Poland's successful show, my friend Dan invited me to return to St. Petersburg, Russia, to do another show. We located a suitable theatre hall—a *dom koltura* or "house of culture."

I had learned that working in other countries required putting my American mindset aside and thinking and doing as the local people think and do. I was learning how to negotiate as a Russian.

My Russian interpreter and I met with the theatre director to sign for the hall, but he wasn't sure he wanted to rent it for a Christian show. He studied the papers and grunted a lot. Finally, he made up his mind, pushed his chair from the desk, and proceeded to do business— Russian style. He pulled three shot glasses from a drawer and poured us a drink. I turned to my interpreter.

"I don't drink."

My interpreter leaned toward me, brows arched, and said, "Do you want the theatre or not?"

I understood. I picked up a shot glass, smiled, and saluted the theatre manager with a nod.

"*Nazdarovye!*" he bellowed, and we three clinked glasses.

He quickly downed his glass, slapped the empty shot on the desk, and then waited for us to follow suit. We repeated the same. Bottoms up!

My interpreter drank and then smacked his glass upside down on the desk. I was next, so I downed my shot. Wow. Reeling from the burning sensation in my throat, I returned my glass to the table-right side up. The manager looked at me, surprised.

"Oh, again!" He poured the two of us another shot.

I looked at the full glass, glanced at my interpreter, and back again to the manager.

"*Nazdarovye!*" he shouted again with a salute. We two clinked glasses and downed another shot of pure Russian vodka. His empty glass slammed first to the desk; mine followed, glass up. Delighted, he poured two more drinks. "*Nazdarovye!*"

Once again, we downed our drinks and slammed our glasses on the table. I choked this third shot down.

Dear Lord!

I was now his newest best friend.

My head was spinning like crazy as I put my glass down. That's when my interpreter leaned over to me and whispered, "Put your glass upside down if you're finished."

Now he tells me!

I flipped my glass over and placed my hand on top. Even the director looked relieved.

I walked out of his office with my head spinning, but thank You, Lord—we got the theatre!

As we moved into the theatre and got things set up, I struggled to get the theatre workers to help. The crew responsible for lighting, sound, and curtains were nowhere around when we needed them. I even tried begging them to help but to no avail. Then I remembered the cultural leverage I had witnessed in other Russian and Ukrainian theatres. Because the workers don't get paid much, they want something more for their services. The female workers desire boxes of chocolates. And the men? *Vodka!*

Against my better judgment, I bought all four a bottle of the eighty-proof fermented potato liquor. Suddenly, these workers were the happiest, most compliant workers. Christ may have turned water into wine, but here in Russia, vodka turned whiners into workers!

We had the theatre; the workers had their bonus, and we did our show without a hitch, seeing hundreds come to Christ, which was the purpose of being here.

> *To the weak I became weak, to win the weak. I have become all things to all people so that by all possible means I might save some.*
>
> —1 Corinthians 9:22

ARRESTED!

Victor invited me to come to Moldova to produce a show that would reach his community with the gospel of Jesus Christ. Of course, I was happy to come to help establish his growing church with a powerful presentation.

I arrived in January 2005 to start production. I stayed at Victor and Emilia's house and caught a dose of reality—Moldovan style.

Every morning, Victor got up at five-thirty, went outside to chop wood, and came back in to start a fire in their furnace. All four rooms in his home surrounded this one lonely beacon of warmth. By six thirty, the house was warm enough for Emilia to wake up and get the children ready for school or church. With no running water in the home, Victor walked a good block away to fetch water from a community well. He carried two buckets and repeated the journey twice more. Two of the buckets were for drinking and cooking, the next two for dishes and the toilet, and the last two just for baths.

But he wasn't finished quite yet. At six thirty, Victor then headed to the barn to feed the pigs and chickens and the other animals, collect eggs from some unhappy hens, and bring them in for the kid's breakfast. After finishing by seven o'clock, Victor settled in his chair by the furnace's warmth and spent time with the Lord preparing for his sermon. One hour before the service, at eight o'clock, he would drive to the church to start the wood furnace to warm the building before the people arrived. Then, because his family owned the only car in their church family, he picked up the elderly or disabled and brought them to church. At nine o'clock, he greeted the people; Emilia led the worship; he preached a fiery sermon, prayed with or counseled church members, then drove the same people home. He'd get home late in the afternoon. I was exhausted and humbled just watching this man of God's total commitment to family and faith in such living conditions.

Everything was going well with the show's production until the Orthodox Church found out. Then the trouble began.

Victor is the pastor of a Protestant church. He helps feed the poor and organize after-school programs for the children, women's programs, and more. And now, on top of all that, he wanted to present a Christian show to the community. That didn't sit well with the city's Orthodox Church. They had to stop this growth by the Protestants in the community.

Moldova used to be part of the Soviet Union and is still run by the Russian Orthodox Church. Until 2005, the government promoted atheism to discourage any church outside the Orthodox Church from taking root. So the Orthodox Church declared Victor's church a cult to deter attendance.

Victor faced many challenges ministering to his community, including finding a theatre to perform in. Protestant churches weren't allowed to rent public facilities. Protestant churches could only meet in private homes. But with most houses being tiny, they couldn't hold many people inside. With this kind of oppressive government, it's a challenge for Christian pastors to grow their churches. In short, we couldn't rent a theatre for our production.

God can make a way where there seems to be no way. I suddenly had an idea.

Cornerstone is registered as a theatrical, not a religious organization, so we went to the cultural hall and showed the manager my documents. He crossed his arms and looked at me suspiciously, "What would this production be about?"

"It's a courtroom drama," I said, stretching the truth. "The people in the show must appear before the judge." I went on. "What makes the show so intriguing is that everyone's case is different. Some of the characters are funny, and some will move you to tears. And based on their answers, the judge determines their fate."

He uncrossed his arms and relaxed a bit, thinking. Then with a nod, he said, "It sounds interesting. Okay, you can do your drama."

Yes! We had the theatre.

I hadn't lied. The play is everything I described. What I didn't say is that the setting of the show is in heaven; God is the judge, and everyone must stand at the judgment seat to see if their name is written in the Lamb's Book of Life.

The cast, who'd been praying for our meeting, were thrilled their prayers had been answered.

We were allowed to move into the theatre one day before the show, so we had our work cut out for us. We had been building our set three weeks in advance and spent most of that day mounting and decorating it. It was complete and cleaned in time for that evening's final dress rehearsal.

Somehow, the Orthodox Church found out. As we rehearsed, a mob of about twenty people, organized by the Orthodox priest, came to tear down all our sets and keep our show from opening. Our cast and crew of thirty, with an average age of twenty-five, defended our scenery from the members of the Orthodox Church, whose average age was seventy-five. We had the age advantage, but we also held the higher ground—the stage.

We lined up along the front of the stage, preventing them from coming up. The elderly Orthodox members made a feeble attempt to storm the stage, but due to their age, they tired quickly. It was an intense encounter but funny at the same time—something you might see in the movies. Our battle was both spiritual and physical. But the old gents winded in a hurry and soon gave up and left.

Praise the Lord; we won that battle! For now.

The next day was the big premiere. We spent it hanging lights, preparing the sound, and finishing the decorations. Time was ticking down, and there was a lot of excited talk about the show in the community. However, the Orthodox Church had regrouped for another confrontation. They stood outside the cultural hall, ankle-deep in snow, protesting our production, trying to intimidate anyone wanting to attend. The priest, in his black robe, wearing a large gold pendant cross around his neck, led the protest. "If you go in there, you're no longer welcome to the Orthodox Church. And if you go there, you will go to hell!"

I couldn't help but think how ironic that sounded because the very message we were sharing was God's love and how to be saved by accepting Jesus Christ as your Lord and Savior. Isn't that what they wanted too? Thankfully, the public ignored their warnings and entered anyway.

The show went off beautifully. The public loved the dramatic message, and at least one hundred souls responded to the altar call, where we prayed with them and rejoiced in their salvation.

The altar call was the last straw. The director over the theatre let the priest know we were praying with people. He, in turn, reported us to the police. I had no idea the trouble this would cause.

The next day I was to fly to Poland and begin a new production. I hugged my dear friend Pastor Victor goodbye and checked in at the airport.

As I was going through security, security agents checked people's passports. I presented my documents. The agent studied it, paused, then called for her supervisor. The supervisor and a guard flanked me and then escorted me to a side room. Apparently, they were waiting for me. My luggage was pulled from their check-in station and placed before us. They looked at me and my gear suspiciously and then told me to open them. They went through every single item, looking for something. They took their time, and as I was looking at my watch, I heard the announcement that my plane was ready to board. I told them my flight was about to leave, but one of the two men snapped at me in Russian, "You're not going anywhere!"

Until then, I had been annoyed. Now, I was alarmed.

They continued to look, seemingly for a reason to falsely arrest me on anything suspicious but found nothing. Then the guards frisked me and found $1,800 in my coat.

They were excited to find my American dollars and accused me of trying to smuggle money out of the country. They asked, "Why didn't you declare it?" At first, I was confused because they were American dollars. Moldovans don't use American dollars; they use their currency—leu—of which I had none. Second, most international travelers know that amounts under $10,000 do not have to be declared.

Even so, they seized my funds.

They took me downstairs to the basement and locked me in a cold, dirty jail cell. Sometime later, the guards returned, bringing four other guards with them, and continued their questioning. None of them spoke English, and I didn't speak Romanian. In Russian, I convinced them to allow me to call my friend to translate for us in Moldovan. I called Victor and explained my frightening situation. He came immediately.

Victor translated. I knew they wanted a bribe. This type of situation was not an uncommon practice in post-Soviet countries. The police pull your car over and insist that one of your tires is too low and you're a danger to traffic, then threaten to impound your car unless you pay them a fine. In this part of the world, bribery is a lucrative business, and corruption runs rampant throughout eastern Europe.

I knew I had done nothing wrong, was unlawfully detained, missed my flight, and now I refused to pay a bribe. The guards already had my $1800 and now wanted more.

I found out later from Victor that there were many agents on my case because they were expecting me to bribe them, and each one would expect payment from the American. They don't get a lot of Americans, so they were expecting a hefty bribe. Their anger rose when they realized they wouldn't get more from me.

"You will not be leaving this country," they threatened. "Your passport will be flagged. You will not escape. Tomorrow you will stand before the police board, and the judge will sentence you to six months for your crime."

They took down all Victor's contact information, and because their jail had no restroom or anyone to watch me, they allowed me to go home with him until my appointed time with the police board.

As I watched the guards divide my money, we asked if we could leave, but they were too distracted over their cut to care and simply waved us out. They didn't even care that I still had my passport.

We grabbed my luggage and returned to Victor's.

I was not used to being treated like a criminal. The experience was so overwhelming to me. I couldn't sleep. I stayed up all night praying and having a pity party. That's when the Lord spoke to me, "Stop feeling sorry for yourself. Get to work!"

It was what I needed to hear. I sat up in bed and confronted the real enemy.

"Devil!" My mind shouted silently into the darkness. "You think you want to stop me? If you keep me here, I will bring as many as possible to the Lord."

Suddenly, a peaceful hush fell over my soul, and I slept soundly.

I woke early and contacted my partners worldwide and asked them to pray about this odd situation where I found myself. My name and problem appeared on church prayer lists around the world. A flood of Christian friends responded with comforting messages. I received thousands of emails from people who didn't know me.

The American Embassy also responded. They must have received information from the border agent's report about an American held for questioning.

At the appointment before the police board that afternoon, a member of the American Embassy was present. Before the hearing, he gave me a lot of legal advice and a care package to hold me over. I was grateful and comforted knowing that they were working on my behalf.

After explaining my side of the situation to the police board, they found it good to continue to detain me for the next three weeks. We all believed they were expecting a bribe from me. A bribe? They already had my $1800.

I'm not one to sit around and wait for something to happen. First of all, I used my Russian language to tell others of Christ. I met two young guards who liked to talk to me. I led them to Christ! I came up with the idea of doing another show while I waited for this kangaroo court to make its next move. I was already in Moldova with all the sets and the costumes at our disposal. So why not go ahead and present another production? I found out from the two young guards if anyone was at the police station over the weekend. Apparently, there was a small weekend crew, and they were part of it. I talked them into giving me freedom over the weekend, and amazingly, they said yes! I'd be free to do whatever I wanted to do over the weekend.

Victor questioned me.

"Aren't you afraid?"

"What are they going to do?" I questioned back. "Arrest me?"

He shrugged his shoulders and said, "Let's do it."

Now that we knew what to expect from the director of any venue, we crafted a plan. We hung posters for our upcoming production in the targeted city. We'd mount the sets the day of the show. After the presentation, we'd drop the curtain while the pastor spoke and gave the altar call. The cast and I would dismantle the sets behind the closed curtain and load them through the back door into a waiting truck. Then we'd drive away into the night before the venue director realized what had just happened and called the police. It was a brilliant plan, and it worked. We did this each weekend, bringing many more people to Jesus.

During these first two weeks of extracurricular ministry, the American Embassy pressed the Moldovan government to hear my case. My embassy said the Moldovan government couldn't hold me for six months. Indeed. The court date was set for the following week. In the meantime, I prayed and prepared spiritually to present myself before the court and accept whatever ruling they might make.

At the court hearing, I was gracious to the judge and didn't say anything critical or defensive. Instead, I told the judge and the court that I loved their country and hoped to return one day, once all this misunderstanding was behind us. Surprised by my kindness and sincerity, her entire demeanor softened. The judge agreed to release me and prevent any hindrance to my reentering Moldova in the future.

My $1,800 were gone for good. However, the judge liked me and extended an invitation to visit with her, should I ever return. Not only did I make another friend in high places, but I was now a free man!

"You intended to harm me, but God intended it for good to accomplish what is now being done, the saving of many lives."

—Genesis 50:20

Kyiv, Ukraine

MATTERS
OF THE
HEART

No one was happier for me to be free than my friends Marc and Kelly. They were concerned for my safety while I was in Moldova, but they also needed me to prepare our sixth production of *The View*. The show went well. Afterward, I was off to Port Elizabeth, South Africa, to begin a new production of *The Promise* with Word of Faith Church. We held auditions and began rehearsals.

A friend invited me on a mountain hike up Van Stadens Pass, so I took the next day off to see the sites. The weather was lovely—crisp air mixed with warm sunshine. We were on an incline and well into the thick of the timber when I had trouble breathing and severe chest pains. I needed to stop until the pain subsided before continuing our climb.

This chest pressure wasn't the first time I'd experienced such pain. For months, I had trouble breathing from the pressure when I overextended myself. I ignored it, hoping the problem would go away on its own. Although I jogged regularly, I wrongly diagnosed my problem as being out of shape.

Friends over the months encouraged me to see a doctor. I dismissed their concerns. "It's nothing," I assured them. "Just a minor problem." My friend here offered the same advice, but I ignored it. I continued to direct *The Promise* and didn't give my chest pain or condition another thought.

We opened our show, and nightly, the show's run went beautifully. In the last scene, the actor Jesus gives the Great Commission line; then, he ascends to heaven. On the technical side, the actor wears a harness attached to some thin cable that is connected to an electronic hoist up over the stage. It's a glorious way to end the performance. However, on the last night of the performance, I was informed that the electric pulley used to hoist Jesus into the heavens wasn't working. I told the crew to ask Jesus, the actor, to simply stay on the mountain after he gave the Great Commission line, and we'd close the curtain in front of him. But the crew insisted that they had an idea, and they promised me that Jesus would ascend. Since the scene was minutes away and I was too busy calling light, sound, and set cues, I had to trust them and give them the go-ahead.

It was time for the final scene. The crew shouted over the radio headset, "He's ready! He's ready!" The lights came up as Jesus stood on the mountain to give the Great Commission line. I looked up from my script and did a double-take. There stood Jesus, the actor, in his glorious robes. But tied around his chest was the thickest rope I had ever seen! It went under his arms and tied behind his back, with the rest of the rope disappearing into the rafters. I felt the blood drain from my face. My jaw dropped. I mouthed "No!" over and over as Jesus gave the inspirational final line of the show.

The music rose to a climax, then as Jesus was supposed to ascend majestically, four guys in the rafters, struggling with all their might, started to pull Jesus—by hand! We saw Jesus go *jerk-stop, jerk-stop*—all the way up to the rafters as the actor tried to maintain a peaceful, triumphant expression on his face.

I wanted to crawl under my director's desk, wait for everyone to leave, and quickly crawl home. Surprisingly, the crowd didn't care. They loved it and roared their approval. The cast received the biggest standing ovation I'd ever seen. Hundreds came forward at the altar call. Afterward, the people gushed about how they loved the show, especially the ending. I was speechless.

The show was a success, but I admit I still cringe (and laugh) every time I think about my crew jerking Jesus around. What was a humiliating experience for me was God's distinct way of touching peoples' hearts. I realized that man's foolishness could sometimes be the very tool that God used to bring people to Himself.

———————•◦•———————

My next ministry stop was Rzeszow, Poland; I met my friends, Pastors Marek and Ewa, as we began work on a new production.

One morning after jogging, I again had severe chest pains. The pain wasn't new to me, but Marek and Ewa were alarmed and encouraged me to be checked out by a doctor. Once again, I dismissed this advice.

The next day, Marek told me he was going to the hospital to pray over patients, and he wanted me to go with him. Once we arrived at the hospital, a nurse with a clipboard came up to me.

"Follow me, please." She led me into an examining room. "Please take off your shirt and wait for the doctor."

I explained to the nurse, "I'm not here to see a doctor. I'm here to pray for patients."

She glanced at the pastor. I looked around and found Marek leaning against the door with a smile. Then it hit me. I looked at

Marek like Jesus must have looked at Judas. My "friend" had betrayed me!

The doctor did several tests, studied my X-rays, then looked at me in alarm.

"You should be dead," he said bluntly with a thick Polish accent.

A shiver went up my spine. The doctor held up my X-ray for me to see.

"You have an artery that is 100 percent blocked. See here?" He pointed to what looked like a branch. "You have a capillary that extends from the artery just before the blockage that goes into your heart. That capillary is taking blood into your heart to keep it pumping. That is why anytime you overextend yourself, you force that capillary to deliver more blood than it can, and if it were to break, you'd be dead."

He went on, "You need to check into the hospital immediately and have heart surgery."

I was in denial. Besides, I didn't want to have surgery in Poland. I thanked the doctor, put on my shirt, and left against his orders.

After a long talk with Marek, we agreed that we should cancel the show. I flew home to the United States and made an appointment with a cardiologist. He told me the same thing as the Polish doctor, then scheduled me for a series of minimally invasive procedures.

I had my required heart procedure. With help from Paul and Brenda, I started going for walks. One short week after the surgery, I was fine. I was back with the living and praising God for an extended warranty on life! I was ready to get back on the road. The moral of this story is: You are no good to God's kingdom if you don't take care of the vessel He gave you. I've since changed my lifestyle and feel better than ever!

I could see how the vision God showed me of ministering to all parts of the world was becoming a reality. Even though I was no longer acting with *The Promise*, my dear friend David Humphrey informed me that Promise Productions would present *The Promise* in Seoul, South Korea, and wanted me to join the tour.

Upon arrival, I met our interpreter, Jae Won Jung, his English name David. We loaded the buses, drove to downtown Seoul, and checked into the Intercontinental Hotel.

We would be performing about a mile away at the majestic Jamsil Olympic Stadium. With the capacity of 100,000, we'd be performing on the biggest stage I'd ever seen—250 feet (seventy-five meters) wide and thirty feet (nine meters) deep. The three-level stage was so massive that the lighting had to be mounted on vertical trusses instead of the traditional horizontal lighting bars.

To the already large cast of 200 actors and the menagerie of animals, a two-thousand-voice choir was added, enveloping the audience with a rich, majestic sound.

It was April, and the stadium was filled with 50,000 enthusiastic people.

I played the role of Satan, which required me to be in many scenes throughout the show. Because the stage was so massive, I had to sprint backstage to make it to the other side of the stage for my next entrance. The excitement of producing such a mammoth production was emotionally and physically exhausting.

———◆●◆———

After the show, we learned that the pastor of the world's largest church, Dr. Yonggi Cho, and his wife, Kim Sunggae, were in the audience. They came backstage to greet the cast. Following them and their staff was a paparazzi with cameras, capturing every move they made. We were excited to be introduced to him but had to be briefed first on proper protocol. "Do not speak unless spoken to, and you offer your hand if he offers his hand first." After Dr. Cho finished speaking to us, he walked in front of me, stopped and studied my costume, and because of my makeup, he commented in Korean and then laughed. I thought he was trying to communicate with me. I didn't want to appear rude, so I held out my hand to greet him. Pastor Cho's smile faded quickly. He looked at me strangely, turned, then walked away.

I didn't fully understand the protocol. You only offer your hand if the pastor offers his hand first, I recalled. Anyway.

Oops.

I was in my dressing room getting out of costume and makeup when one of Pastor Cho's assistants came in. He told me that Pastor Cho would like to talk with me. *Me?* That took me by surprise. As I followed his assistant, I couldn't help but wonder what trouble I might be in having blundered a simple offer of a handshake.

At their limousine, I was pleasantly surprised when Pastor Cho apologized to me for being rude. He invited me to sit in the limousine with him and his wife.

"I was rude to you. It is not the Korean way," he said in English.

How special was that? And how special was it to have the opportunity to personally meet the pastor and his wife of the largest church in the world? We visited and talked for a short while, then they drove away into the night, leaving me standing on the pavement like a starstruck fan watching his hero drive away. Little did I know that God would use this innocent blunder for something bigger.

The next day, at the invitation of Pastor Cho's wife, a small group from our production toured Hansei University. Kim Sunggae remembered speaking to me in the limousine the previous night and wanted to visit more. We talked over tea and cookies. She asked me what I did and perked up when I told her I was a director of a Christian theatre. And I perked up when she informed me that the university was a Christian university and that she was the president. She surprised me when she invited me to come and produce a show with the university students.

We traded contact information. Already my mind was reeling at how quickly the Lord was moving to open another ministry door.

Before our trip to South Korea, Dr. Ron Corley, the president of Promise Productions, had invited me to head *The Promise* in Glen Rose for the summer of 2004. I was honored and looked forward to the opportunity to direct the cast I was once a member of.

Back in Texas, I held auditions and proceeded into rehearsals in Glen Rose.

After only a month of rehearsals and preparations, the show opened its five-month-long season. With a seating capacity of 2,600, we entertained and ministered to thousands each weekend. I was invited back the following year to reprise my role as the director of this anointed musical.

After *The Promise* season finished, I flew to Seoul and was surprised when they greeted me as if I were a celebrity. It started at the airport when a team of bright, smiling youth met me at the gate with a sign and flowers. I also had a new interpreter, Cho Il Hwan, who also took the English name David. David was a student at Hansei. He became a friend and, in time, a producer of some of my later shows in Seoul.

From the airport, they chauffeured me to my apartment near Hansei University. Then at the university, I met with President Kim, who introduced me to everyone as if I were a celebrity. We immediately held auditions and went into rehearsals. Most every day, President Kim invited me to lunch, and we talked. She was incredibly gracious and kind toward me, but I also never lost sight that she wielded a lot of respect and power. She wasn't only president of a prestigious Christian university; she was the first lady of the world's largest church.

During one lunch conversation, President Kim learned that I had been a professional singer. To my surprise, she set up a date for me to sing at their church—Yoido—the world's largest church—with a membership of 850,000. When your husband's the pastor, it's easy to make a phone call and then nonchalantly announce, "Okay, Richard, you're singing Sunday." Wow, that's influence!

Rehearsals for our musical, *Two from Galilee*, went well. Korean actors are incredibly disciplined—quick to learn and dedicated to the task. It was simply a joy to work with them. Before long, the musical was ready. Our show opened, the overture rang out, and the curtains lifted. The public couldn't believe that a university was doing such a professional-level musical. They were amazed, and I was blessed. Pastor Yonggi Cho and President Kim came onstage after the final performance. They were delighted that the show was a success and presented me with flowers and a blue gift. The show had been a trial to see how I fit professionally. I lived up to their expectations. This would be the first of many shows over the years, including a few performances in their church's massive sanctuary. It was an honor to start Yoido's drama ministry.

Pastor Yonggi Cho and wife, Kim Sunggae
Yoido Church, Seoul, South Korea

ADVENTURES
IN
TRAVEL

By 2006 I was ready to tackle the Middle East. I had already done a show in Istanbul a year earlier. I packed my gear and returned to Turkey.

My friend from Seoul, David Cho, joined me to be with Pastors Corey and Rose's church in Istanbul. Together we discussed a future drama and started the ministry wheels in motion.

While in Turkey, David and I wanted to do some sightseeing in beautiful Istanbul. We took a bus to the ancient city of Izmir and caught up with missionary friends from my home church in Dallas, Mark and Michelle. They were kind enough to host us during our three-day, two-night visit.

We wanted to visit the seven churches of Asia Minor where Jesus's disciple John lived out his life. On our journey there, we arrived first in ancient Ephesus and visited the world-famous Celsius Library and the Temple of Artemis, which at one time was considered one of the seven wonders of the world.

When Constantine became emperor, he converted to Christianity and moved the seat of the Catholic Church from Rome to Constantinople (modern-day Istanbul). He outlawed the worship of Artemis and had her temple torn down. Constantine's son, Constantius, became emperor and commissioned the church of Hagia Sophia to be built in Constantinople as a monumental cathedral. He used over a hundred columns from the demolished Temple of Artemis in ancient Ephesus for the cathedral structure in Constantinople. The cathedral was finally completed during the reign of Emperor Justinian I. Today, you can still see columns and parts of the Temple of Artemis (one of the last remaining seven wonders of the ancient world) inside the Hagia Sophia in Istanbul.

At the next stop in Ephesus, we visited the house of Mary (yes, the house of the mother of Jesus). The ruins have been well preserved and have been built upon to recreate the original design of the house, so tourists today can enter it and see how she lived. You'll recall that while Jesus hung on the cross, He commissioned His disciple John to care for His mother. John later moved to Ephesus and built a home for Mary there. This house is where she spent her last days on earth.

Next to Mary's house, the apostle John built a church, which Timothy, the apostle Paul's one-time protégé, would later pastor when John was exiled to Patmos. In the center of the church was a baptismal pool. Typical of such a pool were steps for descending into the holy waters and submerging new believers. Baptism by immersion was the practice in the New Testament church. Despite the ruins, the pool remains.

As fascinating as Mary's home was, the most exciting thing happened at the end of our private tour. Our tour guide led us outside Ephesus to our final stop at the apostle John's tomb. After John's exile at Patmos, he was allowed to come back to Ephesus. Timothy had become the bishop of Ephesus but was later martyred the year before

John arrived. John lived out his final days and died in Ephesus. I had been here to the apostle's tomb once before and knew David would, especially like this.

John's tomb is a large square marble slab with a marker bearing his name. Interestingly, Justinian the I, who finished the Hagia Sophia church, also commissioned St. John's Basilica to be built in AD 548 over John's burial site. The basilica was once a massive and beautiful church but was destroyed in part by the Mongol army in AD 1402 and later by an earthquake, leaving only the four columns protecting this burial site of Jesus's favorite disciple.

It was four o'clock, and most of the tour groups had come and gone, so we had the place to ourselves for another hour before it closed. I asked our guide if John was buried here in the ground.

"No," he said, "John's sarcophagus is in a room under this slab."

Well, wasn't that interesting? No literature hints at that. It just says that this is John's tomb, and that's it.

Our guide didn't know how to get to the underground room, so together, we searched the grounds and discovered a grated metal door. It lay horizontal to the ground and was hidden by knee-high grass. You could see through this metal grated door stone steps descending somewhere into darkness.

The gate had two locks, but we noticed that the hinges were rusty. Curious, we picked up the door to see how heavy it was, and to our shock, the hinges broke off!

David and I glanced at each other in surprise. We were committed, so we swung the gate open, pivoted on the locks, and we slowly took our first steps down these dark, forbidden stairs.

The three of us descended into a long, dark-stone hallway that led us to the room with John's sarcophagus. We stood for a long time gazing at the ancient marble box as if encountering a lost treasure. I had this sudden urge to touch the holy relic housing the disciple that

Jesus loved. Despite my nerves, I managed to keep my hands steady as I videoed the moment. I didn't dare look inside the sarcophagus.

Outside, we blinked against the sunlight and returned the gate to its original place among the weeds. On our somber walk back to our car, I replayed the scene in my mind. We had just been where the apostle John was buried, and I had touched his sarcophagus!

The next day, the reality of what we'd done hit me another way. I felt responsible for the broken hinges and contacted the park. With the help of an interpreter, I told them we noticed that the gate's hinges were broken. I didn't divulge that my South Korean friend and I were the ones who broke it. They said they'd check. I gave them my contact information and told them to contact me when they fixed the gate, as I wanted to pay for it.

A month after our trip, I received an email from the park telling me they had fixed the metal gate and asked if I still wanted to pay for the repairs. Of course, I did. They sent me an invoice, and I wired them the funds.

It's a great joy to know that I not only got to touch the apostle John's sarcophagus but helped to fix the gate guarding his tomb. I had physically touched biblical history!

———————◦•◦———————

Cornerstone was going strong in our seventh year of travel ministry. Over the course of the year, we would stage musical productions in the national theatres in Managua, Nicaragua, Sofia, Bulgaria, plus other shows in Mexico City, Mexico, Cape Town, South Africa, and Cakovec, Croatia. However, 2007 started with some January rehearsals in cold, snowy Ukraine, followed by a fruitful performance in Kyiv. Afterward, it was time to train to Targoviste, Romania, the town where the ruins of Count Dracula's castle still exist. We would begin my second production there.

The train stopped at the Romanian border town of Dorneşti. Despite the cold weather, inside the train was stifling hot. The train offered little except hot tea or instant coffee. I hadn't had a drink of water since leaving Kyiv and was desperately thirsty. I approached the attendant. "How long a stop do we have?" I asked in Russian.

She looked at her watch. "Fifteen minutes." Her native language flowed beautifully.

"So I have time to buy some water?"

She said as if bothered, "Yes, but hurry."

I hopped off the train and ran to the store in front of the station, threw money on the counter, grabbed a bottle of water, then made it back in under five minutes and stopped short.

The train was gone!

A shiver of dread shot up my spine.

In the distance, I watched it chug into the gray horizon of winter. Goosebumps nettled my arms. Was it the cold or that I was stranded in a foreign country, knowing that everything I owned just disappeared in a cloud of snow?

My luggage, laptop, winter coat, and $1700 in my blue coat pocket—gone! My hand instinctively slapped my hip pocket. I sighed a relief. At least my wallet and passport were still with me.

My heart raced while I breathed a desperate prayer. Then an idea came to me. Funny, hadn't I seen this in a movie?

I ran to the street where taxi drivers waited for weary travelers to wake them. I jumped in the front car, jabbing my finger in the direction of the train, and in my best Russian, shouted, "Follow that train!"

Nothing.

I looked to the driver and would have laughed if I wasn't so distraught over missing my train. The man must have been at least eighty years old. His calloused hands slowly placed his glasses on his wrinkled nose, studied me between a few blinks, adjusted his seat, and did a dozen other checks before starting the car.

I bit my tongue. I was losing my mind at how slow the driver moved in light of my emergency. Finally, we pulled away slowly.

"Please hurry." I tried not to sound desperate.

"We must be careful," he nodded a toothless smile, "and safe." He had obviously not seen the same movies I had.

"Sean Connery or Pierce Brosnan never had this problem," I murmured.

"What?" he asked.

"Nothing," I said, with my arms crossed.

Eventually, we made it to the next town, but because of my driver's "careful" driving, we missed the train… again!

After prayer, I realized that I couldn't continue chasing a train. I called ahead to my friend and interpreter, Ovidiu, who was scheduled to pick me up at the Bucharest train station. I told him the situation and gave him my original train's number, the wagon number, and the number to my sleeping quarters in the wagon.

He responded, "I'll bring the police with me."

Whatever for? I wondered.

The next train to Bucharest would be in two hours. Although that's not a long time to wait, it seemed like an eternity without my possessions. I wrapped my arms tighter around me, trying to ease my shivering from the winter chill and wishing I had taken my jacket.

The next train finally came puffing into the station, and I boarded.

Later, when I arrived in Bucharest, I was relieved to see him holding my things. He told me he went to the wagon and explained to the attendant, standing outside the train, that he was there to collect my belongings. He showed her proof of my name and other information on the ticket so she could cross-reference it to me. After a quick, nonchalant look, she said, "I don't know what you're talking about. You must have the wrong train."

Ovidiu knew his culture well and called the police officer over. He confronted her.

"Let him in."

She stepped aside, and Ovidiu hopped in the wagon with the officer following close behind to my sleeping area. When he arrived and opened the door, he found two other train workers rifling through my luggage, dividing up the spoils between themselves and the attendant waiting outside. With the help of the police, Ovidiu recovered everything that belonged to me. I was relieved to know that they hadn't checked my coat pocket. They would have found an easy $1700 to pocket. Ovidiu left with everything while the police officer stayed with the three guilty parties. I'm not sure what happened to them, but I was grateful that I had gotten everything back. My favorite scripture came to mind.

> *The righteous person may have many troubles, but the Lord delivers him from them all.*
>
> —Psalm 34:19

With all my belongings back in my possession, we had auditions and rehearsals and then presented our production in Romania. After our successful drama, I said goodbye to Ovidiu, and I continued my trek to Kazakhstan, an Islamic country bordered by Russia and China. I arrived in the modern and utopian city of Astana, Kazakhstan. I met the pastor and his team there and started production for our upcoming show.

Because the pastors were Christian, the Islamic government refused them three different theatres. I told the pastors, actors, and crew to act by faith and keep rehearsing and building the sets anyway, as I believed a miracle was just around the corner.

A week before the show, we were anxious as the pastors approached the fourth theatre. Thankfully, this theatre manager, fortunately, wasn't familiar with the government's edict against Christian groups, so he approved us and had us sign the contract and pay the deposit. God had just heard and answered our weeks of prayer with a miracle.

We loaded the sets on the morning of the show, but the theatre manager commanded we stop preparations about noon. The manager called the pastors and me into their offices. They had just read the edict.

"Why did you lie to us about your Christian show? You do not have permission from the government, do you?"

A pastor spoke up in our defense, "We had simply asked to rent your theatre for two performances, and you had agreed. How had we lied?" He held out a signed document. "You signed this contract with us, and you are now obligated to allow us to use your theatre since you've already taken our deposit."

With just four hours before the show, he reluctantly agreed. We had to hustle now to get everything ready.

One hour before the show, sixteen police officers and two government officials arrived, warning the pastors and me that if our show was anti-state, anti-Muslim, or anti-Mohammad, they'd stop the show and arrest us.

This threat was a considerable risk, so the pastors asked me if I wanted to continue. I took a moment to pray about it and responded, "I didn't come this far and spend all this time and money putting a show together only to cancel it one hour before. Let's do the show."

They questioned me again, "Are you sure?"

"No," I honestly replied. "So let's hurry and do this."

The public gathered. The hall was packed. I was nervous, not just with the opening of a new show but because they threatened with jail time... again. But God always has a way of helping those who trust Him.

Surprisingly, as the curtain opened on our production of *The Judgment Seat*, the audience gasped at the sight of the angels on stage. Muslims are not used to seeing angels portrayed in shows. Everyone was strangely mesmerized by their presence, including the police and the officials. No one heard the line in the drama that Jesus is "The way, the truth, and the life, and no man comes to the Father except through [Him]." Wouldn't this be considered "anti-Muslim"?

At the end of the show, we received a hearty ovation from the public, including the police. We had a great turnout over the two nights, and although we couldn't do a formal altar call due to the police presence inside the theatre, we were able to pass out thousands of pamphlets outside the theatre on how to be saved.

The pastors treated us to a cast party, complete with a Kazakh favorite: grilled horse with onions and all the trimmings. They presented me with Kazakh clothes, and we took lots of pictures.

What a blessing and an honor.

"I am sending you out like sheep among wolves. Therefore be as shrewd as snakes and as innocent as doves."

—Matthew 10:16

OBSESSION
AND
POLITICS

Over the years, I've produced several shows in Russia. One of the pastors there was an elderly divorced woman who headed the union of male pastors of the city who invited me to produce a show in their city. As I directed, the female pastor had developed a crush on me. The rehearsals went well in her church, but she decided to regularly observe the rehearsals and invited me for coffee or dinner every night after the rehearsal. I was being polite, as she was my host. Over time, she grew uncomfortably close and started making advances, much like Joseph with Potiphar's wife (Genesis 39:7). I could evade her romantic passes but felt very awkward around her. I finally had to confront her and tell her that while I respected her as a pastor, the only relationship between us was of a pastor and a missionary—nothing more. But like Potiphar's wife, she persisted. The show ended, and I left as quickly as possible, escaping another encounter with her. She continued to call me while I was doing shows in Ukraine and later in Europe. I stopped answering her calls, as she just wanted to talk romantically, and I was tired of reassuring her that her feelings were one-sided. Yet she persisted.

I was in beautiful Crimea, near the Black Sea. We would have two productions in Armyansk and one in Krasno-Perekopsk, Crimea. Two years had passed since my "romantic" encounters in Russia.

This female pastor was still stalking me even though I had stopped answering her phone calls for over a year now. Regardless of the country I was in, she was determined to see me again. By now, she was sending threatening emails to coerce me into complying with her wishes. This abuse was getting out of hand, so I wrote my pastors in Dallas, alerting them to the situation and asking them to pray.

On opening night, the house was packed, and the show went great.

We not only had an artistic success but a spiritual victory in the two cities. So it's no surprise the enemy was furious and set traps.

I went on to Sevastopol, Crimea, with Pastor Yuri Feodorovich and began rehearsals. Then, it happened again. I had gotten another call from the Russian female pastor, who told me she would attend our performances, as she wanted to see me.

How did she get my new number?

I panicked and told Pastor Yuri. I told him the situation with this woman was serious, but my concerns fell on deaf ears. He laughed it off, telling me I was being dramatic and that I shouldn't be afraid.

The day before the show, Pastor Yuri got a phone call from "my Russian friend." She told the pastor that she wanted to visit his city. Pastors share housing when visiting, so this wasn't an unusual request. However, he remembered our conversation. He diplomatically told her that this wasn't a good time to visit, as his church had a big event. Still, she insisted. When he stood his ground, she exploded.

"Look, you're protecting Richard, aren't you? I'm coming to see him, and you're not stopping me!"

He finally realized that this wasn't just my fantasy story but a real threat.

All rehearsals and production meetings led to an exciting and sparkling opening night. The people poured into the beautiful theatre, and the hall was packed. Everyone was dressed in their formal best. However, it was difficult for me to concentrate on the show. Pastor Yuri had warned me what might occur and assigned two security guards to be with me. They gave me a code word—*behind*—in Russian. If I heard them use the code, I was to step behind them immediately, no questions asked.

Backstage, I gave last-minute notes to the excited actors. We prayed, and I walked to take my place in the back of the auditorium with my security guards following me. With script and radio in hand, we walked down the corridor. I was deep in thought about how the evening would proceed when suddenly I heard, "Behind, behind!" I was startled, and one security guard pushed me to the lobby wall.

There was the female pastor! She had something under her coat that could be a gun or maybe just an umbrella. They yelled at her, "Get back, get back!" The public was seated inside the hall, waiting for the show to begin. Still, a few in the lobby got a show of their own.

The female pastor yelled at the guards. "I'm a pastor, and I'm a friend of the director!"

They said, "You will not see him tonight, nor are you allowed in the theatre."

She yelled at me, "Richard! Tell them who I am! Richard! Richard!" I didn't even want to make eye contact as they ushered me away.

Other security came running and detained her while my two guards led me to my place so that we could begin the show. I was a nervous wreck, but I was grateful they were there.

The curtain went up; the people applauded, and we began. I forced myself to concentrate on the show, but I kept looking over my shoulder, wondering what had transpired out in the lobby. The show went well, but afterward, my guards didn't allow me to stay in the theatre. They ushered me out and got me safely to my hotel. I don't know what happened to her. The following year, while I was in the USA, she called me my Texas home number. How she got it, I have no idea.

"I'm coming to see you. We have to talk."

I hung up on her. I called a friend in Florida and asked if I could stay with him and his family for a time while I tried to elude this crazy stalker once and for all. I hopped on a plane to Florida and breathed a sigh of relief, feeling a special kinship with my biblical pal Joseph.

Not so romantic, I know. I'm loved—just not in the way I ever envisioned.

———◆••◆———

Politics and religion are rarely a good mix. Here is a case in point: in November of 2008, I was in Cakovec, Croatia, putting together a Christmas show.

I had just delegated the nativity roles of Joseph and Mary to two of the best singers at the audition: Bojan and Ena, two young actors from a Catholic church who sang and acted well. They were both perfect for the roles. In addition to looking like the biblical characters—or at least as we imagine—they were humble and worked hard.

The day after our first rehearsal, the pastors of the Protestant Church we were working with wanted to speak with me. They informed me that they didn't want both Joseph and Mary to be Catholic. In their theological minds, two Catholics were too many for what was supposed to be a protestant church event. Therefore, they decided that Bojan would have to go. Talent had nothing to do with their pharisaical decision.

I opposed this decision, defending Bojan's honor and place in the show.

This decision merged religion and politics—sheer illogical lunacy.

After the rehearsal the following day, the actors milled around talking.

The pastors showed up.

"Did you cut him?"

I could feel my anger rising.

"This is your decision. You do it."

Angry with me that I didn't cut him, they called Bojan into a side room.

Bojan came in all smiles, as he didn't know what he was walking into, but we knew. I looked on in disgust, praying against this bigotry. A pastor spoke up.

"Bojan, we're afraid we no longer need you. We're dropping you from the show."

Bojan looked confused. He shook his head. "But why? Did I do something wrong?" He looked to me for an answer but saw the same confused look. "I'm sorry. I'll do better. Please, tell me what I did."

The pastors held their ground. "Please, you must leave."

Downcast, Bojan, justifiably upset, left quickly and quietly.

Fuming, I ran out of the building after Bojan and found him visibly shaken, confused, and crying by his car. I stood beside him, lost in embarrassment, thinking about how to comfort a wrongful rejection, but found little explanation.

"Bojan," I said, "I'm sorry. I had nothing to do with their decision. It was wrong. I know."

He looked at me with wet eyes.

"What did I do, Richard? Someone tell me what I did wrong."

"You did nothing wrong, Bojan." I struggled for words. "Politics are ugly and shouldn't be in the church. It's not right. If you can, forgive them. You're incredibly talented, and you'll do great things for God if you don't give up on Him."

It wasn't much consolation at the time, but it was the only solace I could offer under the awkward situation. Bojan thanked me with a hug and drove off into the night. At that moment, I was so ashamed of the church for allowing religious hypocrisy. I had to take a short, fast walk to calm down.

We cast a protestant actor to the liking of the pastors in the role of Joseph and spent the following weeks in rehearsals. We opened *Two from Galilee*, and the presentation went beautifully. The next day, we performed a matinee followed by another flawless evening show. Everything went exceptionally well, which made me happy, except for the embarrassing episode that happened with Bojan.

Bojan competed in Croatian Idol and won the following year. He was now a national teen sensation and a musical celebrity in Croatia, with every reason to hate what the church had done to him. Yet, he remained humble. Years later, he proceeded to rejoin one of my shows, *Les Misérables,* in the city of Varazdin, where he brilliantly played the role of Marius. I'm so grateful to young men like Bojan. Humility, forgiveness, and determination are keys to success.

———◆●◆———

My twenty-second world tour took me to Lima, Peru, where a young missionary from Spain invited me. Angel was our coordinator. He had heard of me and wanted to produce a show in Peru. He introduced me to a room full of pastors. After introductions, they whisked me away to Carabayllo to assess the region where we would stage the show. We talked about the auditions and the production.

With the help of Rey, my host from a previous show I had directed in Madrid, Spain, and Sonja, one of my magnificent dancers and a talented choreographer from Dallas, the production was going to be an amazing art festival of music, pantomime, dance, and drama.

The show would be performed outside, so we set up the stage, the lights, the sound, and the decorations. Our workers labored all day in the hot sun until six o'clock, an hour before the show. With everyone on stage, we prayed and then promptly started at seven o'clock.

The show opened with 500 people in the audience. By eight o'clock, the seats filled to around 3000, and people continued to pour in.

Sonja's extravagant dances and Rey's witty skits went well, and then we presented *The Judgment Seat*, followed by an altar call. By the end of the show, we ended up with 4000 in attendance, and more than 400 souls came forward to surrender their lives to Jesus.

What a night!

Day two was busy re-setting for a new performance later this evening. We opened to cheers from the public as we presented the preshow concert with dances and mimes. Again, *The Judgment Seat* was the main attraction, so we saw another 4000 attentive patrons hanging on to the message the show generated.

We were all tired from the night before but exceptionally happy with how beautifully the two shows went. Again, we saw 400 people come to the Lord on night two. The preparations had been tense, but it's incredible what can be accomplished when we work for the Lord's agenda and not for our own.

> *"This is to my Father's glory, that you bear much fruit,*
> *showing yourselves to be my disciples."*
> —John 15:8

Varaždin, Croatia

MY OWN JUNGLE BOOK STORY

Five hours and 1700 miles later, I landed in Managua, Nicaragua. Pablo, an actor, producer, and friend, came to pick me up at the airport, and together, we headed down the road. We hadn't gone far when he suddenly remembered he needed to go by the church to pick up something.

The church was dark, and the doors were locked when we arrived. Pablo fished the keys from his pocket, then fiddled noisily with the lock. The door swung open, and before he could flick the light switch, the lights came on, followed by a roar of voices.

"Surprise!"

My wide eyes adjusted to a church full of cheering people, along with a small band strumming out traditional Nicaraguan music. The cake on the table in the corner read, "Welcome Back, Richard!" Pastor Milton had arranged this wonderful moment.

My mouth fell open. My eyes grew wide. *Should I laugh or yell along with the welcoming party?* Being a good guest, I indulged in the cake and party snacks.

Only later, while staying in Milton's home and seeing how desperately poor he was, could I fully appreciate the extravagant party he had thrown last night. The shower in his home was the size of a small three-foot by three-foot (ninety centimeters) closet crudely made with cinder blocks and a cut-off garden hose protruding from the wall. The water's only temperature? Cold. I had to brush my teeth at the outdoor sink under a bunch of palm trees.

We met with several churches that were thrilled to participate. Milton had recruited seven churches to participate, and they were happy to be a part of our theatrical outreach.

Out of 200 who came to audition, we cast seventy-five actors. It was one of the largest casts I've ever had in Nicaragua. We would be performing *The Hiding Place*, the dramatic story of Corrie ten Boom. We built a four-story Dutch home on stage that was converted into a concentration camp for act two.

We held our show in the beautiful National Theatre Rubén Darío. Every night we played to a full house, and the people were moved by the message of forgiveness.

I thanked the actors and crew, especially the Pastors Milton and Pablo, for making this production a reality. Despite how poor Milton was, he continued to invite me back to Nicaragua, and thanks to his efforts, over the years, we have done dozens of productions together. I'll always be grateful to Milton, his faith in God, and his vision for Cornerstone for Nicaragua.

———— •◆• ————

Before leaving Nicaragua, I contacted the pastor of a "large church" in Panama City. The pastor invited me to come and present a show for the community. I have them answer basic questions to confirm that they have the size and people to be able to host a theatrical production. He answered affirmatively. He told me they were organized and had a "rented theatre" and "actors waiting to participate." This would be great. I wouldn't need to fuss with finding and negotiating a venue or advertise for auditions.

I landed in Panama City, picked up my blue luggage from the luggage carousel, and went to the airport lobby looking for the pastor. I waited... and waited.

No one.

I tried calling his cell phone.

No answer.

Hours went by. *Maybe he thought I'd be coming tomorrow.* It was getting dark, the airport was empty, and I needed to find a hotel for the night. I'd try to connect with him in the morning.

The next day, I returned to the airport—continued waiting and kept trying to call and left text messages. Finally, a pastor's friend arrived to tell me that the pastor lived in Colon, about two hours away, and advised me to take the bus.

I caught a taxi to the bus station, then a bus to Colon. Two hours later, I was dropped off at the bus stop called La Feria, where he had instructed me to wait for him. I got off the bus and retrieved my luggage. I noticed nothing more than a bus sign sticking out of the ground in the middle of... a *jungle*. There is no station, no bus stop, or even a bench to sit on. Just... a *jungle*. This had to be a mistake.

Again, I waited for the pastor.

Nothing.

I called him multiple times, but there was no answer. Hours later, I was still standing with my luggage around me, texting him, and waiting helplessly in the hot and humid forest, slapping at mosquitoes, pacing and praying as I watched two cars pass by, hoping he was in one of them.

The sun was going down, and my cell phone battery was dying from calling the pastor, who refused to answer.

I was alone. But I was not alone. Out of the bush and down from the trees, forty wiry little monkeys advanced toward me. Even though they weren't large, there were many and curious enough to inspect me and my luggage.

While they were playing tag with my suitcase, pulling and tugging, I tried to be the alpha male, waving my arms and yelling at them to scare them away. At first, they were afraid, but then more monkeys came. I didn't know what they were planning, but I didn't like the looks they gave me. I prayed, but it was far from humble. I yelled.

"Lord, I am not spending the night in the jungle with the monkeys. Help me!"

Suddenly, I spotted a car in the distance.

Finally!

Shooing the monkeys back, I positioned myself and my luggage in the middle of the narrow road with a bonus of a group of monkeys who now considered me and my blue luggage their friend. I wasn't. With the sun almost set, no car was getting past me this time.

The car came to a stop, eyes wide at my presence with the monkeys. Inside were two families with kids crammed in the back. I told them about my desperate situation.

"We have no room," the driver said, eyeing the back seat.

That's when I went into director overdrive.

"Yes, you do!" My words came out a bit too forceful. "Put these kids on your laps, put one of my bags here, and, in the front seat, I'll hold this bag in my lap."

Understanding my dilemma and seeing the night closing in, the family was sympathetic to my request and rearranged the seating to accommodate me: everything but one oversized suitcase fit. So I got in the car and, with my arm hanging out the window, grasped my luggage, and we drove away into the dusk packed like sardines. *Adios, monkeys!*

Providentially, the good Samaritans in the car knew of the church and knew the pastor lived next to the church. We arrived, and I thanked the good Panamians profusely and turned to find the pastor's house. Neighbors pointed me to his home.

I knocked on the door, sweaty, wrinkled, achy, and smelling of the jungle. A child answered. With weary eyes, I looked down.

"Is your father here?" I asked politely in Spanish.

"*Sí.*" She opened the door further.

The pastor sat comfortably in a chair, reading a newspaper. He looked up, shocked to see me standing at the door, my blue linen shirt drenched in sweat with my blue luggage hanging from my hands.

Fuming, I understood he'd had no intention of picking me up. He knew I was coming by bus, but he saw fit to ignore my calls for two days and leave me abandoned in the jungle for some unknown reason. Now, he just stood there, and we looked at each other in silence without a greeting. He didn't know what to say or do. I tried to hold my tongue, but my "greeting" came out a little curt anyway.

"Where is your bathroom?"

Without saying a word, the pastor pointed down the hall. I looked to his wife.

"Where are the towels?"

She gave me one, and I went into the bathroom to shower. I came out in clean clothes, still holding back my ire.

"Which room will I sleep in?"

I was given the silent, pointing finger again.

"In the morning," I concluded, "we'll talk. Good night."

The mosquitoes were eating me alive in the house, but I was too tired to care. Exhaustion overtook me, and I soon fell asleep.

After a sweaty, humid night, I woke at seven o'clock and showered again. The pastor's wife had breakfast ready. After some forced pleasantries, I asked the obvious question.

"Why weren't you there to pick me up at the airport or meet me at La Feria? You said you would."

He shrugged as if it wasn't a big deal.

"I changed my mind about doing the show," he confessed. "Because it was so late, I thought when you arrived, and no one was there to pick you up, you would give up and just leave."

Give up and just leave? Who thinks like that? Absurd!

If there is one reason why perhaps the Lord has called me to represent Him worldwide is that I am ferociously tenacious. Translation: I never, never give up. If he thought I was going to quit and go away, he was learning he chose the wrong man.

It turned out that everything the pastor told me from the beginning was a lie. He didn't have a large congregation. He didn't have funds. He hadn't rented a theatre. I could only imagine how horrible his work ethic would have been. I grabbed my bags and took the bus back to Panama City.

I had every reason to leave Panama, but the Lord placed it on my heart to stay and do a production. Panamanians needed the gospel, and it was apparent that the pastor who asked me here had no intention of helping deliver the good news.

I called Pastor Milton, and he agreed to fly in to help me. We prayed and decided to move ahead with plans to do the show independently. My tenacity had kicked into overdrive. However, we would need some miraculous help.

Peru had paid me nothing. Nicaragua also had paid me nothing, and now I was in Panama, and I didn't have two *centavos* to rub together.

My bank account registered zero. I had about $150 in my pocket. How would we pay for a theatre? Scenery? Costumes? Promotions?

We have no host, no support, no actors, no housing, and no money for this project. Even Milton was dependent on me. All I had was a mandate from God to do a show.

If ever I needed to operate by faith, it was now.

Then God kicked into God mode, and a few miracles started happening. The only theatre we could find was the National Theatre. We were able to book the theatre for the dates we needed. The theatre's director gave us a rental price of $2000 for two days but assured us we didn't need to pay now.

"We'll sign the contract and worry about payment later."

That was good because I had nothing to give him right then.

Around dinner time, Milton and I were walking to the hotel when we passed by a church. We heard the worship team in rehearsal and went in to speak to the pastor. Inside, we talked with a kind young lady, Lorena, the church administrator. I told her I was from the US and was in town to do a Christian show and wanted to have auditions using the church's actors. She seemed genuinely interested.

"When do you need the actors for the auditions?"

"Tonight," I said.

"Where will the auditions be?"

"Here?" I asked sheepishly.

Her eyes got big. "I'll have to speak to the pastor. He's getting ready for the service now. Stay for the service, and you'll be able to speak with him afterward."

We thanked her and added, "We're tired and haven't eaten. We'll grab a bite to eat, and we'll be back in a couple of hours."

We left, had dinner, and came back to talk with her.

"What did the pastor say?"

She responded as if she didn't believe it herself. "He said… okay."

Yes! Now that's favor. The Lord knew our situation, and since He was the One encouraging me to stay, He was opening doors as only God can do.

We didn't waste time. With rehearsals started, we focused on advertising, building sets, and sewing costumes. Funds were miraculously coming in from friends in the US.

Lorena, the church administrator, started helping us too. Not only was she acting in the show, but she also helped us find an apartment that belonged to a member of the church. She spoke to the proprietor on our behalf, and the owner was gracious enough to let us use it for free for one month. We had no furniture, but we were never happier. Lorena brought us pillows, blankets, towels, and a few other items like pots and pans.

Milton and I visited and spoke at various church services promoting the show, while Pastor Luis's church passed out all their flyers and hung posters in the area. Now, all we needed to do was to continue to prepare for the show and wait for God to bring the people so we could present Him with a new harvest of souls. More funds came in.

We had the funds now to pay the deposit for the theatre. I called the theatre director each week, but he kept saying, "You can sign the contract and pay the deposit later."

But now, "later" was the week of the show, and I was worried. The show was coming up fast, and the contract needed to be secured and finalized with the deposit.

Finally, the day of the show was upon us, and we needed to move in. It would be tough to set up everything in one day, but I was organized and had a setup plan. We could do this.

We were advised that the theatre would be opened by 8 a.m. to begin setting up for that Saturday evening's performance. We met at 7 a.m. with the workers at the church, loaded up the van with sets, and were at the theatre by eight. We went to open the doors, but they were locked.

We called the theatre. No one answered.

At 10 a.m., the other workers arrived along with the sets that needed to be mounted and painted.

Still no answer from the theatre. *What is it with Panamian leaders and phones?*

Finally, I reached the theatre director. The man I thought earlier was such a friendly Christian turned out to be a conniver. He told me the show was canceled because we never signed the contract. We? Didn't sign the contract?

I had been trying for weeks to pin him down to give him our deposit and sign a contract, and he knew it! He'd continually insisted, "Don't worry about the contract; we can sign it later."

We're stranded outside the theatre with tons of sets and workers eager to prepare for the evening performance. We presold 1000 tickets, and those ticket holders would soon arrive and expect to see a presentation. With all the time, energy, and money already spent, I couldn't cancel the show. My tenacity was growing. I wouldn't cancel the show, even if we had to hold it outside.

I called for prayer and told everyone that if we ever needed a miracle, it was now. After praying, by faith, I decided to use the time wisely and got everyone busy finishing and painting sets outside the theatre in the sun.

As we continued to pray and work, I discovered one of the actors was involved in politics. He volunteered to make some calls. Before long, he got a call back... from the vice president of Panama! The vice president made some calls that must have struck a nerve with someone at the theatre. Finally, at three thirty that afternoon, the keys came out, and doors swung open.

It's interesting how prayer and faith can do the impossible. We were moving a mountain.

With fewer than three hours to mount everything on stage, the workers did their job while I helped with the sound and lights. By 6:30 p.m., we let the public in as we worked zealously behind the curtains to make sure the sets were ready.

Against all odds, the curtains opened, and *The Judgment Seat* started at 7 p.m. with me in a sweat-soaked t-shirt and jeans. Hygiene would have to take a back seat this evening.

Considering we hadn't had either lighting or sound practice or a final dress rehearsal, the show went well, with 120 Panamanians giving their hearts to Jesus!

I congratulated the cast and gave a few notes for the next day's show, and we all went home feeling victorious. As I packed up to go home, I was summoned to the theatre's administrative office.

The theatre was now demanding an inflated payment of $3000. The director initially told us he would tell us the rental price when we signed the contract, but he said it wouldn't be more than $2000. What happened? He was furious we had embarrassed him with the vice president of the country, we later found out.

I took Pablo and Milton with me, and we gave the two staff workers from the theatre an earful. They had treated us horrifically, and they knew they were to blame.

We only paid $1500 of the $3000. In truth, we didn't have any more than $1500. They didn't know it, so I needed a reason not to pay more. I told them I didn't trust them.

"What if we come tomorrow and the doors are locked again?" I questioned their integrity. "We'll pay you the rest tomorrow night, *after* the show," I bluffed.

But they knew we were right and accepted the $1500… for now. They still wanted the entire $3000. I prayed earnestly for more ticket sales tomorrow night.

The next morning, I was still on cloud nine from the last night's miracle. We arrived at the theatre early and finished all that we couldn't complete the day before. When the actors arrived, we prayed and opened the last performance. It was beautiful, and the actors did a great job. We saw at least 100 more people come forward for prayer.

Now the dirty work. As the cast and crew took down the props, we were once again summoned to the office and talked to the director's assistant, but she had an attorney trying to force us to pay the $3000. The attorney was intimidating and forceful, and worst of all, she lied and yelled a lot.

Pablo wasn't fazed and did most of the talking, challenging the attorney's demands. Gently but firmly, he stated our case.

The attorney said, "You know, I'm recording everything you're saying, and I have a recording that you're refusing to pay."

"Ma'am," Pablo said, "I wasn't born yesterday. I'm a telecommunication specialist, and you're not legally allowed to tape me without my consent, and I don't give it."

Caught in her lie, she attempted to save face.

"I am, indeed, recording you!"

Pablo stood erect, crossed his arms in front of him, and looked her in the eye. "Okay, let me hear it."

"Well," she hesitated, then pointed the finger at me. "I have your director recorded. He had called earlier telling us we had to meet today to settle the payment because he was scheduled to leave Panama the next day."

Pablo chuckled with a sly smile. "That's called voicemail, which can be altered. It's not a recording. Besides, he didn't promise to pay any specific amount."

She continued her demand for an additional $1,500.

Now it was my turn.

"Please show me in the contract that we owe you $3000, and we'll pay it."

Her bottom teeth raked her upper lip, smearing her bright red lipstick. You could see her eyes shifting back and forth in agitated thought. She had nothing. Not even a signed contract.

Game over! We agreed to pay an additional $500 for a total of $2000, the original price, citing that their lack of professionalism in opening the theatre to us on time hurt the quality of our show. She knew we were right, accepted the settlement, and left in a huff.

The truth was that all I had left was $700, and I had just given her $500. We gave Milton, who was most in need, the remaining $200.

I've discovered as a Christian that you can have the victory if you simply don't give up. It's the devil's job to discourage you. The enemy can't stop you, but he will try to make the situation so complicated that you lose hope and finally say, "I quit!" That's when he wins. Don't ever give up on your hope, and don't ever give up on God.

> *"No one will be able to stand against you all the days of your life. As I was with Moses, so I will be with you; I will never leave you nor forsake you."*
>
> Joshua 1:5

DUELING
SHOWS

In December of 2009, I had invitations to direct two Christmas shows—one in Seoul, South Korea, and the other from Colleyville, Texas. Because I love Pastor Yonggi Cho and Pastor Ricky Texada, I said yes to both. What was I thinking committing to Christmas shows for two churches simultaneously on two different continents?

I began in Dallas and held auditions for *Two from Galilee*. We gathered an excellent cast and began rehearsals. Ten days later, I left the Dallas cast and packed my bags. Fourteen hours later, I landed in Seoul. I was taken straight to casting from the airport to audition for new actors.

With the rehearsals well underway, I taught the choreography to the different cast groups. The day before I was due to fly back to

Dallas, I directed a complete run-through rehearsal. Back at my apartment, I packed until two in the morning.

When you travel from Asia to the US, you can leave Korea at 10 a.m. and land in Dallas the same day at 2 p.m. Taking advantage of that, I rested for three hours upon arrival, then drove straight to rehearsals at my church.

By now, I had been awake for twenty-seven hours and was exhausted but excited to be back.

The morning started with a production meeting. I met with the sets, props, costumes, lighting, and sound teams. After I led the meeting, I received an ovation. Now, who gets applause after a production meeting?

"What's this for?" I asked.

"We're amazed how organized you are. Two shows on two continents? Who does that?" Pastor Ricky responded on behalf of the team.

Now that's nice! I have learned that no ministry can ever rise higher than its ability to organize. No matter how talented a leader is, he will never succeed if he doesn't know how to manage his time and his finances.

I met nightly with my talented actors, and we staged all of act two; then, it was time to get back to Korea. Fourteen hours later, I was back to my Korean rehearsals. In my absence, the cast had worked on their parts and looked pretty good. I was so proud of them.

Tim, my actor playing the role of Joseph in Dallas, had come with me to Korea to help me carry two trunks of costumes. Tim was in his early twenties and looked like a teen heartthrob. Not only is he handsome, but he's White. Koreans consider fair-skinned people to be good-looking. Couple that with his blue eyes and light brown hair; you have a Korean triple threat. So, when I introduced Tim to my Korean actors, the girls giggled and mobbed him, greeting him "Korean style." It was amusing watching him take it all in.

We were ready to move rehearsals into the theatre. This would be our first run-through with costumes, lights, sets, props, curtains, stage, platforms, etc. These rehearsals are typically long, as we work through unanticipated problems.

We had our final dress rehearsal the next day, and the run-through went well. With thirty minutes left, we organized the curtain call.

On the first day of the show in Korea, I went to the theatre at 10 a.m. to resolve problems with the sets. The angel's apparatus wasn't flying. The backdrops weren't rising and lowering in time for the scene changes.

I gave some notes to the actors and let them get into costume and makeup.

That evening, the audience's excited talk before the show was deafening. Backstage, we prayed. Then the overture began. The audience can simply sit back and enjoy the show during the performance, but I am as frantic as ever. While one scene plays out on stage, I'm behind the curtain, anticipating the next scene and every potential technical problem, trying to avert disaster. I'm physically and emotionally exhausted by the end of the show and the curtain call.

With the show over, I could relax and have a little fun. At our cast party the next night, I invited Tim to do his role of Joseph in English while Mi Ae, my Korean Mary, did her role in Korean. The cast loved it. Suddenly, it was a paparazzi moment. Everyone pulled out their camera and took pictures and videos of the duo's every move.

The next day, Tim and I loaded the van with costume trunks and headed to the airport, where several cast members bid us a fond farewell.

———◆•◆———

Many hours later, Tim and I touched down at Dallas/Fort Worth airport. We were home and caught our second wind.

The next day, I resumed rehearsals with the local cast and dancers. It was time to load into the church auditorium. Everyone knew what to do and worked on their assigned duties.

Showtime!

The auditorium was filled with familiar faces. Contrary to what you might think, a home show is more intimidating than a production in another community or country. The logistics may be more challenging in an unfamiliar theatre, but a home show takes place before friends and family, the board of directors, pastors, and others you know and whose opinions you value.

The curtains opened; the show began, and I was pleasantly relieved to see it going amazingly well. We finished, and the curtain closed. The actors scrambled in place for the curtain call, and... the curtain wouldn't rise. We tried again as the audience applauded but to no avail.

I quickly got the stage manager to send the pastor on stage as the audience finished applauding, so it looked like it was all part of the program.

Pastor Ricky came forward and gave the altar call while my crew tried frantically to fix the curtain backstage. When Pastor Ricky finished with the altar call, I stepped in front of the curtain, ready to explain to the unsuspecting audience that the curtain wouldn't open for the curtain call. Just as I was about to speak—the curtain opened! I then said, "Ladies and gentlemen, the cast of *Two from Galilee*! The actors all scrambled back in place, and we did the curtain call before the cheering crowd, who never knew the disaster we had just diverted.

The next night, we'd have a big, beautiful cast party. The cast presented me with a gift, and we watched our show, which had been videotaped earlier. It was so much fun watching it with the actors. They laughed, cheered, and teased each other.

As I watched the actors enjoy themselves, I fondly recalled how the Lord had allowed the American musical to be as successful as the Korean musical. Both went perfectly, and so ended the two-continent performance run. At that moment, our Lord's encouraging words came to mind.

> *Jesus looked at them and said, "With man this is impossible, but with God, all things are possible"*
> —Matthew 19:26

Afterward, I drove to Austin to be with my aunt, uncles, and other family members for the holidays. We all pitched in and cooked a big Montez dinner while enjoying each other's company and wishing all a Merry Christmas. After a beautiful dinner together, I wanted to speak to my uncles about the Lord. Both were approaching eighty, and I wanted to ensure they were ready for eternity.

I spoke first with Uncle Frank. We had a long talk about the Lord, and I asked him if he wanted to accept Jesus into his heart, and he said yes! So I led him in the sinner's prayer. What a privilege to pray with him. My other uncle was not ready yet to pray. Perhaps soon.

What a fantastic way to end 2009 with my biological and spiritual families and an uncle gloriously saved. What a blessing!

I began 2010 with high hopes of conquering Africa. I flew to Lagos, Nigeria, based on an invitation from a great missionary friend from my home church in Dallas.

In many airports, passengers wait in an orderly line to go through passport control. Not here in Nigeria. A sea of people pushed and shoved to get to the passport desks.

My host, Pastor Uche, came to pick me up and took me straight to their church, where I met Pastor Wole and Bukola, the senior pastor and his wife, and his staff. We talked a bit, then went into the service already in session. Entering their stage, I was taken aback to see 3000 people in a room designed to hold 1000. It was quite a sight, seeing a crowd of Nigerians this size getting into praise and worship.

When I was introduced, the people stood and cheered. I felt blessed to worship with them. I was so mesmerized by their exuberance that I couldn't worship; I could only watch in awe. I spoke, and the people were very responsive. I could only imagine what the show would be like with this much excitement.

After the service, Pastor Wole invited me to his office with his wife. They sat on elegant couches. I sat opposite them and talked about the upcoming show—the typical routine when preparing for a production in another country. Nothing unusual until there was a knock at the door. An assistant opened the door, and a young couple, dressed in a smart suit and a formal church dress, were allowed to enter by security. They took off their shoes and set them aside. Then, on their knees, they proceeded to crawl to the pastor.

I thought this might be a joke of some sort for a moment. But what shocked me was when they reached the pastor, still on their knees, they took his hand and humbly kissed it as if he were a king.

Similar interruptions happened four more times during our session—another well-dressed couple entered on their knees, kissed the pastor's hand, and spoke with him in reverential tones in their native language. If this was a Nigerian custom, I wasn't sure I could get used to it. A fascinating cultural difference, for sure.

I unpacked and put everything away at the hotel while waiting for my assistant, Segun. We took a taxi to church and prepared for the auditions. I noticed that there were large portraits of the pastor in every hall and office. We got the casting area ready. Far more Nigerians wanted to audition than we could accommodate in one day.

At the end of the day, Segun announced, "That's all for today. Go home. Come back tomorrow."

I'd never treated actors with such a cavalier attitude. But it didn't seem to be a big deal for anyone. Just another cultural difference I'd have to get used to.

Back at the hotel, we ordered dinner. I had a sandwich and soup, while Segun had a Nigerian favorite: pounded yams and Eforiro—a mash made of fish, meat, and other questionable things unfamiliar to my American palette.

The next day, auditions continued. Another large crowd assembled, so we were geared up to see them all. With the excellent pool of talent, we cast the show, printed the scripts, and then met with the actors. I gave them an overview of the play, and we read through the script.

After the read-through, some actors told me they felt the power of *The Judgment Seat* and wanted to get saved… again. I prayed with several actors to recommit their lives to Jesus that night.

Afterward, I was taken to see some potential theatre halls. Had we been doing a horror show, any one of them would have been perfect; they were that scary. I had never done a show in halls as bad as what we had just witnessed. I would have to settle for the church sanctuary, which was certainly nicer than these places.

Working in Lagos felt like running in mud. I struggled with all my might yet hardly moved forward. The Internet, for example, is incredibly slow. In America, I can send several messages in ten to fifteen minutes. In Nigeria, the same job takes around three to four hours. I discovered the best time to use the Internet was between four and six o'clock in the morning. I set my alarm and accomplished many things before breakfast.

Solomon, one of my actors, was blessed to be a part of the show and wanted to have a traditional Nigerian shirt and pants, a Buba and Sokoto, made for me.

The following Sunday, before the service, I was asked to say something to promote the show during the service. I wore my Buba and Sokoto, which got a huge ovation when I took the podium. We showed a promo video, and then I greeted the people in their native Nigerian language, Yoruba, and was rewarded with a roar of approval from the congregation. I'm sure I butchered their language. They loved me for trying. I invited the cast to come to the front and asked the pastor to pray over them.

———◆◆◆———

Many Nigerians assume White people are rich—a concept they've gathered from Western movies and culture. I recall walking down the street and Nigerians calling out, "Hey, White man!"

"Why do they call out to me like that, Segun? I'm not White."

He countered, "Here, if you're not Black, you're White."

White? Of course, I don't see color. It's just strange to a Nigerian to see a White person living like them. So they were calling out mainly in fascination.

———◆◆◆———

As the performance dates drew closer, we built sets, designed costumes with what we had, and rehearsed lines and scenes. I spoke with the lighting people about the price to rent lights and brought them down from $5200 to $1300. We talked to the sound man, and instead of $2600, we got an unthinkable reduction to only $260. And the pipes to hang the curtains? From $520 down to $180.

Despite this miraculous low price for this equipment, the church kept putting off the payments, and now, it was the day of the show.

I asked the assistant pastor almost every day if he could speak to the senior pastor for the money needed to pay the vendors. We had a show tonight, and we were all waiting in the hot morning sun for the assistant pastor to come back with the finances, but he never came. The pastor is seen as a king. So the assistant pastor was afraid to bother Pastor Wole unannounced and instead left out the back door.

Now, I, the guest artist, was left to enter the chambers of the esteemed senior pastor and beg for money. I was not going to kneel and crawl in like others would've done. Instead, I went straight to his office, knocked, walked in without waiting for a response, and announced:

"Pastor, the lighting, sound, and curtain men are outside and want their money. We've haggled them down from $8320 to $1740—the lowest we can go. That's more than a $6,500 reduction in prices. This is a great blessing, and we'll have everything we need for the show. But if these people leave, they won't be coming back for tonight's performance."

He frowned but understood. "Let me think about this."

Ten minutes later, he called me back to his office and handed me a stack of Nigerian currency. We paid the vendors, and we were now moving quickly to make up for the lost time.

A few hours before the show, we began our run-through. The cast's hard work and diligence paid off; they had their parts down. But tech problems lingered.

I was concerned, yet I had a sense of peace with the situation. If Nigeria had done nothing else for me, it had prepared me for chaos. I started staging the actors' curtain call, and now they were ready for opening.

We had less than one hour to prepare for *The Judgment Seat* and met the volunteers who arrived to decorate. Time was of the essence, so I told the actors to go get into costumes and makeup while I gave the volunteers a list of things to work on. With hundreds of tasks and time racing, we closed the curtain and let the public be seated. We worked behind the curtains—the public never knowing we weren't ready. We were all hot and exhausted, but it was time to start the show. This would be the actors' first time with mics, lights, curtains, sets, and costumes. How could we possibly do it? I gave out last-minute notes, prayed, and lifted the curtains.

Ready or not, it was showtime!

Somehow, the cast and crew managed to do everything as if they had practiced all day.

The Nigerian people are emotional and freely express themselves. Each time they got a glimpse of heaven, they applauded, and they were visibly shaken when someone went to hell. This was one of the most interactive audiences I had ever experienced. Best of all, half of the audience, half, came forward for salvation.

The Lord came through in a unique, beautiful way and blessed us with a fruitful show.

For the next four nights, my team enthusiastically presented *The Judgment Seat*, and each night the crowd loved the show. So captivated were they that at least 1000 thirsty souls came forward after each performance for either salvation or to rededicate their life to Jesus. That was over 5,000 souls saved in less than a week.

The last night would be our best show. We took our bows and smiled for cast pictures. Pastor Wole prayed over us; I said my heartfelt goodbyes. I would miss these wonderfully sensitive people, especially my dear friend and assistant, Segun, but it was time to leave Lagos and set my sights on Kenya.

Colleyville, Texas, USA

KENYA— SUCKER PUNCHED

Kenya is a land of beauty. Tourists have their choice of numerous scenic sites. They typically stay in guarded compounds with manicured trees and professional landscaping that hide the high-security walls. Within these compounds are well-maintained roads, five-star hotels, and high-end shops and restaurants where safety is paramount, allowing tourists to freely walk down those streets. They are reliable tourist sites that provide massive revenue for Kenya, so they must take good care of their international guests.

Then, there's the other side of Kenya. A poverty-stricken society without an effective welfare service for the poor, sick, deformed, and mentally disturbed. Begging, stealing, and manipulating are a way of life for a desperate society suppressed by the corrupt government. It was to this side of Kenya that my inviting pastor lured me with a deceiving spirit.

The pastor, a friend of a friend, reached out to me on my social media page. I was naturally cautious. I explained the usual Cornerstone requirements to work with a local church for the stage space, talent, and financial support to produce one of my shows. I asked the pastor pointed questions and requested photos of his church and congregation. I received pictures of an attractive building with lovely families worshiping the Lord. All looked great, and his website was impressive, so I accepted his invitation.

From Nigeria, I flew directly to Kenya. In contrast to Nigeria, the airport in Kenya was modern and orderly. The passport station was professional, and the luggage carousels were organized. It's where the tourists arrive before they're whisked away in air-conditioned mini busses. I met my host, Pastor M., and three young men who led me out to the hot, crowded parking area to an old, dilapidated car.

The trouble began on the drive from the airport to Nairobi. After pleasantries, I asked, "Where will I be staying?"

"Wherever you want," Pastor M. replied.

Wow, how nice that they're letting me choose!

Upon arrival in the downtown region, he said, "You're paying, so just choose what you can afford."

Choose what I can afford?

"Um, Pastor? Before we confirmed I would come, part of our written agreement was that you would provide housing for me, which you agreed to."

He looked at me nonchalantly. "But we can't afford to pay that from our church budget."

I never sign an agreement or contract with any pastor or church. Pastors would be offended if I asked for a signed contract, assuming I didn't trust them. Ninety-five percent of the time, a pastor's word is sufficient, and everything works fine. This just so happened to be a church on the five percent side.

We found as upscale a hotel as I could personally afford near the church. I explained to the manager that I'd be staying five weeks. We arrived at a price I could afford.

Because I arrived early, we went out for a typical Kenyan breakfast: fried bread with avocado, boiled white corn, and hot tea. We went to the national theatre where we would be putting on the show. To my dismay, the theatre was in terrible condition. In place of theatre stage lights, they used regular light bulbs; the theatre seats were torn and in bad shape. And this was the national theatre?

Later that day, we would go to the church to hold auditions. Wait. Where was the big church, and where was the audition hall? We were in the center of the ghetto in a crowded marketplace on the third floor. The audition room was a concrete box with an iron gate for a door. Being the optimist, I assumed they were meeting here for the artist's convenience. We began auditions. Only three were from Pastor M.'s church of the thirty that auditioned. During the audition, actors asked, "Will we be paid?"

I explained that this was a ministry, and we were all volunteers, including me.

After a long day of auditions, I finally cast the show. I then asked Ken, my assistant, if we could go to the church to see the rehearsal space. He said, "This is the church." This concrete box? The room held ten to twelve plastic chairs and no sound system. There were no doors or windows—only an iron gate with a padlock.

I felt my blood pressure rise. I clenched my teeth, trying to hold back my anger, and paced through the small room, arms crossed. My mind was a turbulent cloud of unbelief. I turned to the pastor, who was arriving after the auditions.

"Big hall?" I signed air quotes. "Pastor M., you assured me before I came that we'd have a hall large enough to stage a full-scale play."

He shrugged. "Well, it's big to us."

I released an exasperated sigh. It was painfully apparent that Pastor M. and his church had no money, no space, and no people to support a show. How was I to pull off this show?

————— ◆●◆ —————

Ken and I printed, collated, and bound the scripts before our first rehearsal the following day. Orientation went well, and then we met the actors in this third-floor concrete hall and read through the script. The actors seemed to enjoy the read-through, but afterward, they again questioned me, "Will we be paid for this?"

"No," I confirmed. "As Christians, this is our service to the Lord. We're doing this show to reach the people of Kenya with the gospel."

I had never paid actors and wasn't planning on starting now.

Back in my hotel room, I decided there was no way that this church could do a show. They had no lodging. No funds. No rehearsal space. No support. Too few actors. And now these amateurs want money? No way, I quit!

I had a hard time praying about the situation I was caught in, but I did anyway and would decide in the morning after I slept on it.

I asked Pastor M. if we could find a better place than the national theatre in the morning.

"Oh, we can't afford that place. I thought we could use our church."

His church? That tiny space. Was he kidding?

"We had an agreement," I reminded him, "that you were responsible for providing a forty-foot (twelve meters) long by thirty-foot (nine meters) wide stage to put on a show properly. I need a stage that's even larger than your entire church."

"If you want the national theatre," he said, "you'll have to pay for it yourself."

The pastor lied to me to get me here, knowing I would never have agreed to come if he'd told me the actual situation. I finally admitted how I was feeling.

"You promised me a proper theatre, a big church to rehearse in, a congregation large enough to choose actors from, plus financial support for the production. You've delivered zero percent of your promises. So knowing you didn't have anything I asked for, why did you invite me?"

He stepped forward, and with all gall and sincerity, he asked, "Can you give our church $1,000?"

For a moment, I was speechless. I studied him to see if he was serious. He was.

"Pastor," I leveled with him, "I'm a missionary, and I live by faith, and I already can't afford to pay for my own accommodation while sponsoring this production."

"Come on. You're an American!" He looked at me with a sly grin as if I might be pulling his leg.

A wave of holy anger was building inside me. I was furious but held my tongue, turned, and walked away without saying a word— my mind smoldering.

———— •◆• ————

In the morning, I went through the motions at the rehearsals. Little was accomplished, and all the actors continued to ask for money.

After rehearsal, I stormed into my hotel room and shouted again, "I quit!"

I started packing. Enough was enough. I didn't bother folding my clothes; I just threw them in my luggage. Then I felt the Lord nudge me.

"Richard, stay and do the show. Whatever country you go to, you always bear fruit. If you leave Kenya now, this will be the first time you won't bear fruit."

"But Lord," I fast-balled a wad of dirty socks in my blue luggage, "how will I pay for all this?"

"With your own funds."

"Oh no, Lord. I only have $5000 in the bank."

"Stay. In each country you go to, you produce spiritual fruit. If you leave Kenya, you will have produced no fruit."

I sat hard on the bed, thinking… praying… then finally surrendering. "Okay, Lord. I'll trust You to provide."

I took a deep breath and went into rehearsals the next day. Soon the actors were saying they were hungry or thirsty. I had a bottle of juice with me. They started asking me for a drink. What was going on? Were they so poor that they couldn't afford a meal or water to drink?

I gave Ken some money, and he returned with juice for everyone. Now maybe we could continue? Then someone said, "We don't have food in our house."

This became a habit at every rehearsal. I gave them the benefit of the doubt, as I never want to see someone hungry. I surmised that the least I could do was bless them with something to eat. So I bought food and drink at every rehearsal and gave Ken money daily to purchase something for the actors.

After a day of rehearsals, I returned to my hotel room, exhausted. I settled in, expecting to open my computer, go over my notes, check emails, etc. Where was my blue laptop? I scoured the room, but I couldn't find it anywhere. It was gone along with my USB drive, iPad, and everything about my ministry. I had been *robbed!*

I went directly to the manager at the front desk.

"My computer and iPad are missing from my room. They've been stolen!"

"Yeah," he shrugged. "You should be more careful."

More careful? *More careful?* Everything was locked safely in my hotel room.

Someone on the hotel's staff had something to do with the theft. What in the world is wrong with these people? They think nothing of asking for money or robbing you.

It became apparent that the manager would be of no help, so I'd have to solve my own problem. I grabbed my keys and went straight to the print shop and printed several reward signs promising $50 for the return of my "lost items." I placed them around the hotel and prayed for someone to call.

———◆•◆———

Around three o'clock in the morning, I was awakened by a phone call.

"Hello?"

"We 'found' your things. We can come to your room. Do you have the money?"

"I'll meet you in the lobby."

I didn't want strangers to come to my room. What else might they do to me? A half-hour later, I met two men in the lobby. They made up some bogus story that they were cleaning, found my items, and saw the note. Then the guy who stole my things dared to ask me if I could help him get to America.

"Sorry, no!"

I gave them the reward money and bid them goodnight. Back in my room, I locked the door, flopped on my bed, closed my eyes, and exhaled in relief.

I was so thankful that the Lord heard my prayer to have my electronics returned, but I was simultaneously furious that Kenyans were taking advantage of me at every turn. I'd have to inconveniently carry everything of value with me from now on.

The following morning, I went to a store to buy some items for my hotel room. As I waited in line to pay for my goods, the woman in front of me laid her purse on the counter so she could pack her groceries in a bag. Just as she was doing so, a young man grabbed her purse and took off running. The lady screamed. "My purse!"

But no one did anything, and the boy quickly disappeared into the city. I realized this was a way of life for Kenyans. I realized that I would have to keep my bag secured between my knees when I sat to eat from now on. But even then, I didn't feel safe.

One day, as I was having lunch at a small restaurant, squeezing my bag between my knees, two men stared at me across the room. It was enough to make anyone feel paranoid. I paid for my lunch and then hurried out the door, scrambled behind the restaurant, and hid. Sure enough, the two men came out looking for me. Watching them search the street, I slipped back inside the restaurant, had some tea to quiet my nerves, and put some distance between those men and me before going to rehearsal.

———◆◆◆———

Everywhere I walked, I noticed poor, homeless, or crippled people on the streets. Once again, as in Nigeria, I stood out for my skin tone. People grabbed my arm, shirt, or bag and said, "Hey, White man, give me money!"

This happened twenty or thirty times a day. Even Pastor M. continued asking me for money to fund his church. I was overwhelmed with so many empty hands reaching out to me. I was already paying for the production and feeding actors daily, and now he wanted me to support his church.

Pastor M. asked me to preach to the ten people in his congregation. I reluctantly agreed. After all, I do have the heart to win souls for Christ.

Another pastor heard of me and invited me to preach and promote the show at their church. The following Sunday morning, I made my way to the church in the middle of another ghetto. Surrounded by dirt streets, the church, like the houses, was a tin shack with a dirt floor. Chickens, dogs, and dirty, barefoot, but adorably cute children, ran through the dirt streets.

Inside the church, on a couple of rickety benches, sat three poor women with six children. My heart suddenly ached for them. These people needed a different ministry than mine. They needed food, clothes, and the hope of the gospel.

I preached an encouraging sermon to the few and left as soon as I'd finished speaking. But the paradox was that I was so discouraged—the conditions I had to live and work in, the people in constant need, the lies, the deceit, the thefts, and my bruised pride. I vowed again to cancel the show. Back at the hotel, I flung my suitcase on the bed and tried again to pack. Once again, the Lord reminded me of my mission. I put my suitcase away.

I had been writing friends and ministry partners horror stories of my experiences in Kenya and requesting prayer. Finally, a breakthrough. I met a local pastor having breakfast at the hotel café where I stayed. We talked, and then I asked for his help. He was sympathetic and agreed to help us with the show. He sent his youth pastor, who was full of joy and optimism. He offered help in any way, including providing some of his youth to help us backstage. I was so grateful. I left our meeting encouraged for the first time since arriving in Kenya.

Back to rehearsals. One of the actresses wanted to "talk to me." By now, I had learned what that meant. Since I arrived, actors have wanted to "talk to me" about helping them go to America to become a celebrity, study in America, give them money for their sick aunt or blind cousin, etc. I never promised anything, only assured them I would pray about what I could do. This actress wanted me to support her financially to go to America to be a star.

Rehearsals were going well. I gave some money to Nelly, the church's volunteer secretary who would become one of my only friends whom I could trust, to buy snacks for everyone. However, some of the actors weren't satisfied with the food and drinks at every rehearsal. They now wanted me to pay their bus fare too. I reluctantly agreed.

With the production finally and fully underway, sets being built, lights rented, costumes made, decorations purchased, and the actors fed, my funds were dwindling quickly. I went ahead and paid off the total amount for the theatre and then investigated renting curtains.

Posters were printed and paid for, but we couldn't display them without paying someone to post them and then pay for the space where they were placed. It's all a game, an expensive game.

———◆•◆———

I needed a break and decided to see the local sights. As I walked and photographed the scenery, I had to continually deny the locals asking me for money. Then a young man approached me.

"You're new here. Let me show you around."

I shrugged. "That would be nice, but I can't pay you anything."

"No problem," he said, smiling. "I like to help tourists. Come on."

The young man seemed friendly enough. I remained leery but let my guard down and obliged his offer.

We walked and talked as I pointed out a few sites and asked about them. Strange, he didn't seem too interested in answering my questions and instead made calls on his cell phone, speaking in Kenyan. I didn't give it much thought at the time. After all, this was a free tour guide. A little farther, we came across an old church.

"Well, isn't that a great church!" I stopped and admired it. "You know, I'd like to go and peek inside. Take some pictures."

The young man looked at his phone and then kicked a little dirt with his toe. "It's not a good idea; it's getting late. Hurry with your pictures."

"If you need to leave, that's okay. I can finish touring by myself."

"No, no. I'll wait. There's much more I want to show you. Go. Hurry!"

I went inside and saw that the pastor was there. After a short introduction, he looked out the window at my guide.

"Why are you with that young man?"

"Him? He volunteered to give me a private tour of your city."

The pastor crossed his arms and said, "You know"—he nodded with his head—"that 'tour guide' of yours is planning on mugging you."

My brows arched in surprise. The young man was much smaller than me and had no visible weapons I could see. The pastor went on to explain.

"See, he is on the phone right now. He will guide you through a nearby vacant lot where his friends will pretend to mug the both of you. They will take both his wallet and yours and all your other things in your backpack. Your 'guide' will act as if he is a victim too, but later, he will meet back up with his friends. They will give him back his wallet and then split the money and items among themselves that they've stolen from you. They've been doing this with other tourists."

Again, I couldn't believe the rampant deceit in this country.

I thanked the pastor very much for his insight and then went out and told my "guide" that I would be staying longer at the church. And just as I had expected, he didn't like it.

"Why are you mad?"

"I just want to show you some things," he begged. "Just ten more minutes, that's all."

"Sorry, no. It's time we go our separate ways."

He was furious and spewed a few curse words at me, then left.

After he left, the pastor was kind enough to drive me back to my hotel. Before I got out, he advised, "Stay inside."

Back in my room, I thanked the Lord for bringing me in touch with this pastor. The only way I could keep hope alive was to start a countdown until the time I left Kenya.

Many who minister in Kenya work with churches that house them in safe hotels or tourist or church compounds and then bus or taxi their guests to ensure their safety while they minister. They accompany them to safe tourist sights and restaurants. I didn't have that luxury. I was an independent ministry that was conned. I was on my own in the streets with no protection except the Lord's.

The week of the show coincided with the political referendum. The night before our final rehearsal, I was trying to sleep, but there was rioting in the streets, making me fearful for my life. The following day, I looked out the hotel window and couldn't believe what I saw—two dead men in the street! Unconcerned, people walked around them as though it were an everyday occurrence—such turmoil in this country. My heart went out to the families of those young men.

Later that day, we took all the sets to the national theatre. Some workers showed up, and we were busy getting the stage ready. By evening, we had our first run-through. It was rough, but we got through it.

The actors were getting bolder wanting money. I didn't know if I had enough to pay the workers to build the sets, mount the lights and sound, let alone pay the actors. I made it clear to the actors. "No pay!" I did, however, give the cast and crew four complimentary tickets so that they could invite their friends or family to the show.

On the morning of the first show, we filled two taxis with all the props and decorations and unloaded them at the national theatre. The lighting and sound showed up late, so we were busy programming lights and doing sound checks.

We managed the last run-through dress rehearsal. Then I shooed everyone off the stage, closed the main curtain, and let the public in. We fed the cast, and I gave them some last-minute notes and prayed.

The emcee introduced the show. To my relief, the show went well. One of the new pastors did the altar call, and fifty people came forward. Fruit! Finally, there was fruit for the Lord! This is what my outreach was all about.

After the show, I had to pay some people. I was down to $775 total cash on me. My bank account was empty. I paid the food ladies ($80) to feed the cast and crew that day. I took Ken out to eat ($10), then took a taxi to the hotel ($2). Now I had $683.

———◆◆———

I checked my finances and calculated how I would pay everyone. The next day, Ken and I met for lunch ($10).

My USBs were missing… again! I tried to put it out of my mind and focus on that evening's show. Another taxi drive ($2) to the theatre, and at five o'clock, the actors arrived. We fed them, and I paid the food ladies again ($80).

While I searched for the crew to set up for the show, I found our crew outside scalping their complimentary tickets in front of the theatre. Corruption runs rampant, even among those who call themselves Christians.

After the show, I took the taxi home ($2). I was now down to $589 in my wallet.

———◆•◆———

On our show's third and final day, I woke sick to my stomach and feverish. My chest felt heavy. Ken picked me up, and together, we took a taxi ($2) to the theatre. More crew workers asked for money. I could hardly wait to get out of Kenya.

We got ready, and everyone showed up on time for the food. I paid the catering ladies again ($80). We prayed and opened our last show.

We had our biggest crowd, and happily, they loved the show. We had the altar call, and seventy came forward for a total of 180 people in three nights. Finally, we were finished!

I had everyone help take everything down and out of the theatre. But everyone still wanted money. The two camera operators wanted to be paid. They had agreed to $40 each, but I paid them $50 each instead, thinking they'd be happy ($100). Instead, they countered. "What about all the work we did videotaping?" they complained. "We expected more."

Grrrrr…

Next, I thanked and paid my assistant Ken ($300), the average monthly salary in Kenya, and his assistant Erick ($100), who worked only part-time. They took the money and simply left. I expected a more gracious goodbye, but why would I expect more here?

I was now down to only $7; $2 earmarked for the taxi to my hotel and $5 reserved for the ride to the airport tomorrow. I had to laugh; I would be making it out of Kenya with $0 to my name, but at least I'd owe nothing—*Hallelujah!*

———◆•◆———

Despite all the troubles, we had a beautiful show. I was sicker than ever. Runny nose, coughing, fever, and an upset stomach. Even so, "We did it, Lord!"

Usually, when I say goodbye at the end of the show, the actors swarm me to hug me and thank me. Not here. Everyone knew I was leaving, but instead of farewells, they swarmed me with their typical requests, but more forcefully.

"Can you help me financially?"

"Can you pay my fare?"

"Can you help me go to America?"

Not even one thanked me for putting on the show.

Not a single "Thank you for coming. See you later. Stay safe. Come back again!"

None of the niceties one expects. They just take, take, take. And when I couldn't give them anything, they turned their begging into anger.

"You paid everyone else? The sets, the lights, the costumes, the sound. Everyone got paid, but we didn't?" I tried to explain that they got food, drinks, bus fare, and complimentary tickets.

Then they shocked me. They mugged me.

"Give us what's in your bag!"

They were convinced it was filled with money, but it was only my laptop, passport, clothes, and $7. I had to fight them off physically.

And then it happened—I got sucker-punched in the face, resulting in a black eye. Then from behind, a girl dug her fingernails into my face as if to hold me, while from the front, some guys continued to tug at my bag while hitting me in the chest, trying to pry it from my grip. This left some serious bruises and scratch marks, some that bled.

These people were supposed to be Christians—*my actors!* I think some were defending me, but I couldn't tell in the chaos of the mugging.

With great effort, I tore my shoulder bag from their hands and ran to the taxi, jumped in, and locked the doors.

"Go!" I yelled to the driver. He took off in a trail of dust with them chasing me, just like in a B movie. Unbelievable.

Far from the theatre now, I hustled to my hotel room. I couldn't pack fast enough. I was on the verge of an emotional or mental breakdown. I had a runny nose, and I was coughing uncontrollably. Now I had a black eye, bruises, and scratch marks on my bleeding face. In the hollows of my room, I yelled silently at the Lord.

"You told me to stay! You told me to help these… ingrates! I did what You asked, and look what they did to me. They robbed me. They beat me. They almost killed me. And that's what I get for bringing the gospel to them?"

My voice was hoarse. My shirt was soaked in sweat. I was so sick and feverish that my head felt like it would explode. I held my hot head between two sweaty palms. My eyes welled in tears. I was drained.

"Good," I heard the Spirit of the Lord deep in my soul. "Now you know how my Son, Jesus, felt."

> I want to know Christ—yes, to know the power of his resurrection and participation in his sufferings, becoming like him in his death.
>
> —Philippians 3:10

I slumped to the floor, took a long breath, and broke down in tears. I had never thought I'd suffer as Jesus did. Christ went through everything I went through, but His ordeal was worse, deeper, more horrifying… and then they killed Him. Numb, I sat and wept on the hotel floor. I finally understood what the Scripture meant; Jesus's disciples suffered for His name and were even martyred for the cause of

Christ's kingdom. Was I exempt from that? Not if I'm serious about my calling to follow Christ.

I rolled into bed but couldn't sleep. I tossed and turned all night due to my fever and pounding headache. I got up twice, afraid I'd missed my flight. I was also terrified someone had stolen my bag. In my sleep, I kept dreaming that someone was attacking me and woke again gasping for breath. I was suffering from post-traumatic stress syndrome.

Finally, I dressed and finished packing at five o'clock in the morning. I took my last $5 and paid for a shuttle to take me to the airport. My money was gone. I couldn't buy breakfast at the airport or a bottle of water, but I didn't care—I was leaving Kenya at last. I got my boarding ticket and boarded to Johannesburg, South Africa. Despite my fever, scratches, and a black eye when the plane left the ground, I cried in relief. I'd never been happier to shake the dust of a country off my feet.

And the God of all grace, who called you to his eternal glory in Christ, after you have suffered a little while, will himself restore you and make you strong, firm and steadfast.

—1 Peter 5:10

GOD
REWARDS THE
OBEDIENT

Four hours after leaving Kenya, we landed in South Africa. Finally! Familiar territory. Even though I had a black eye, bruises and scratches on my face, and a red nose from blowing it so much, I was thrilled to be back in South Africa. I was still trying to shake off my experiences in Kenya as I went through passport control.

"Welcome to South Africa, Mr. Montez. Where have you come from?"

"Kenya." *What must I look like to everyone?* I thought to myself.

"May I see your vaccination card, please?"

"Vaccination card? I don't have one."

I could see the agent's eyebrows lift.

"I'm sorry, Mr. Montez, but you can't enter South Africa without your vaccination card."

"But I've been to South Africa many times, and I've never been asked about a vaccination card."

"You must have always flown in from the USA or Europe, which is okay. But Kenya is considered a yellow nation, and yellow nations have high incidents of malaria and yellow fever."

"But I feel fine," I said as I wiped my runny nose with a tissue.

She looked at me with a half-grin, then handed me over to a young man who escorted me to the health quarantine area.

"Which airlines did you fly in on, sir?" The young man asked.

"Kenya Airways." *Sniff.*

He studied the screen.

"The next flight back to Kenya leaves in four hours... ."

My mind screamed, *Nooo!*

My heart raced, and my bloodshot eyes revealed my stress. He tried to calm me.

"It's okay, Mr. Montez. The flight will be free. Yellow fever or malaria are transmitted through mosquitoes, and if one infected person is allowed into the country, a whole pandemic could arise, causing nationwide problems. You can understand that our only line of defense is to stop people at the border."

I interrupted him.

"Please, I can't go back. I have no money, and there's nothing there for me."

"I'm sorry, but you can't stay here."

I was at my wit's end. Not only had Kenya sucker punched me while I was there, but now it wanted to take a final swing at me. I prayed a quiet but desperate prayer.

"Lord, please help me; I can't go back to Kenya!"

The health agent typed for a while and then perked up. He must have come across my occupation where it stated I was a missionary.

"So you're a Christian," he declared. "So am I. What do you do?"

"I share the gospel through theatrical plays." I tried to control my trembling voice.

He returned a smile, and we talked a bit about those who come to Christ through my work, including my past work in South Africa. He paused for a moment.

"I could lose my job over this. Wait here, and if anyone comes, don't say anything."

I didn't know what was happening, but I knew God was working. I started praying earnestly. It was the longest ten minutes of my life. When he finally came back, he handed me my passport.

"It's stamped, Mr. Montez. Go," He whispered. "If you go through those gates on the left, they will take you around the cameras that monitor fevers."

Then he gave me a reassuring look. "Welcome to South Africa, Mr. Montez." He held out my passport.

I took my passport, and I thanked him. I walked away fighting tears and praising the Lord. I felt like the apostle Peter must've felt when the angel guided him past the guards and out of the jail and into freedom in Acts 12:9–10. The powerful arm of the Lord is still opening prison doors.

I transferred to a domestic flight and flew on to Durban for a short stay. Charmaine, the worship leader for Durban Christian Centre, where I had directed a musical a few years back, met me. We hugged and then she saw my face.

"Goodness! What happened?"

I briefly filled her in on the situation in Kenya, omitting most of the details.

In her car, I finally got a look at myself and was embarrassed by what I saw in the mirror. When we arrived at her house, my former actors were there to surprise me… but they were the ones who were surprised—by my appearance. Still, they loved me as we caught up.

It was refreshing to be with people who were so giving for a change. Before I arrived, they spoke of giving me a gift but couldn't decide, so they took up a love offering instead. They could not have known that I was penniless. Their gift of $100 might as well have been a million. They hugged me goodnight.

Before retiring to my room, Charmaine treated my face with creams and ointments.

The following day, Charmaine took me to the airport for my flight to Cape Town. Expressing my heartfelt appreciation for her hospitality and facial, we hugged goodbye.

I was met at the airport by David, my former actor, now the drama director for his church. He greeted me with, "What happened to your face?"

David had scheduled me as the keynote speaker at an actor's workshop. While self-conscious about my scarred face, the actors appreciated the practical artistic study and thanked me. And no one asked me for money!

Afterward, I was treated to a stay at the Victoria and Albert, a five-star luxury hotel on the waterfront overlooking Table Mountain and Robbin Island, compliments of his church. I indulged in the spa facilities, where I was treated to another facial.

David brought along a friend of mine, Grant, the worship leader at their church. He has been my right-hand man in past theatrical productions at their church and had become a dear friend. I think we hugged for what felt like an hour! They took me to the airport, hugged me and gave me an envelope. It contained about $450 in South African rand collected from the actor's workshop the previous night. What a blessing! God was paying me back for what I had spent in Kenya.

I flew to Port Elizabeth and was met by good friends: Philip and Yvette. They booked their luxurious boutique suite in their hotel for me, which featured a chandelier and hot tub in the middle of the room. After settling in, they invited me to their new steak house restaurant, the Cattle Baron. Overwhelmed by their kindness, I confessed that even though I would love to come, I had already booked the evening with some friends.

"Invite them all!"

I reconnected with many friends over Chateaubriand, baked potato, and a salad. After dinner, everyone ordered dessert, but Philip and Yvette said they'd order for me. My eyes grew big when servers brought out one of every dessert on the menu and placed them before me.

I returned to my luxurious suite, where I tried to wrap my head around all the extraordinary kindness I had received here in South Africa. The Lord rewarded me after going through the shadow of the valley of death.

As I prepared to leave South Africa, Phillip approached me. "Yvette and I have been touched by what happened to you in Kenya." He handed me an envelope. "We want you to have this."

In the car, I opened the envelope and found $700. With the earlier gifts from the workshop and my friends in Durban, I had $1250 in cash, and over the next few days, other funds were gifted to my ministry back in the USA, totaling more than I had spent for the production in Kenya.

Lesson: You can't outgive God. God is faithful and true to those who trust in Him. Once again, this mantra rings true in my life:

"You will succeed if you just don't quit."

During my long flight from South Africa back to America, the Lord asked me a question about my time in Kenya.

"Richard. Who's the *least* in the kingdom"?

"I suppose the orphan children or the elderly, both of which have to beg for bread just to exist."

"They are not the least because it's human nature to have compassion for children or the elderly. Even the godless have a natural compassion for them. Who are the least? The least, My son, are those who deserve blessings the least. Although you do great or sacrificial things for them, they are people who do not appreciate it or can even attack you.

"My son, it's difficult to serve people like that. You need supernatural compassion for them. My Son, Jesus, was the ultimate example. When they nailed Him to the cross, He said, 'Father, forgive them, for they know not what they do.'"

He said, "You have been serving others out of your own love and compassion. I will teach you how to serve out of supernatural love from now on. My love will flow through you to empower you to love and serve even the most unlovable."

I cried as I flew over the Atlantic. My African tour was a master class in learning to follow Christ and love supernaturally and unconditionally.

Directing — Glenrose, Texas, USA

CREATIVE
SOLUTIONS

I travel so much that it's essential I have a home church where I'm held spiritually accountable and spiritually protected. The Lord had a solution for me.

I heard about a new church in the Dallas suburb of Southlake, Texas. On an invitation from a friend, I went to Gateway Church one Wednesday evening and experienced some anointed praise and worship. The message by Pastor Robert Morris was spot on. I felt the Lord urging me to join. I wanted to make sure it was the Lord, so I said a quick prayer and put a fleece before the Lord.

"Lord, if I can speak to both the mission's pastor and the senior pastor tonight, I'll know it's Your will for me to join."

Gideon's fleece before the Lord (Judges 6:37) asked for a supernatural sign from God. With the giant size of this church, my fleece would also require a supernatural move.

After the Wednesday evening service, I went to the stage to speak to the pastor, but I was stopped by ushers and told to make an appointment. *Okay, so far, this isn't going well.*

I asked where I could find the mission's pastor, but no one knew. I left a little disillusioned. As I approached my car, I felt the Lord say, "Go back in and join."

So I dutifully obeyed, with or without a fleece. I found the new members area and told them I wanted to join. They were closing, but they stayed open for me while I filled out the membership information. I then asked for the name of the mission's pastor so I could call him and set an appointment to meet. The lady helping me pointed behind her.

"You can talk to him now. He's right over there."

What? I turned and walked straight to Pastor Juan Constantino as if the Holy Spirit was leading me. We had a great talk, and he invited me to lunch later that week. That was cool! I surmised that one out of two men I had asked to meet was half the sign I asked for, so I felt pretty satisfied. I said good night and started down the lobby. As I rounded the corner, *boom!* I physically ran into Pastor Robert.

"Oh, excuse me," he said. "I need to be more careful."

I was amazed at God's ability to honor my fleece by guiding His people to meet me. I introduced myself as a new member and shared my ministry with him. We talked for about ten minutes; then, he prayed over me. I thanked him and floated out to my car as in a dream. I had found my home church!

I flew from the US and arrived in Duga Resa, Croatia, where I cast actors to participate in a new production of *Joseph*. But something strange was happening. At every rehearsal, we lost one or two cast members. We had lost so many actors that we were in danger of canceling the show. However, the Lord gave me a creative solution: Croatia is a small country, and the cities are close enough that distance is not a concern. I have done *Joseph* in many towns in Croatia in recent years. I got an idea: recruit those who'd already performed in the recent shows in their towns. Soon we had all the roles filled.

I taught the remaining Duga Resa actors: 25 percent of the cast needed. The day before the performance, 75 percent of the veteran actors arrived from as far away as Slovenia. It was a wonderful reunion of my Croatian actors. Since they all knew the show, assigning everyone their position and reviewing the dances was easy.

It was time to open the production. All the schools in the area were excited to see an American musical. We were booked solid for the next couple of days; two morning shows daily for the kids and one each evening for the adults.

Our first show opened at ten o'clock for the first through third graders. They were like rivers of children, coming from their school busses, filling up the theatre. We prayed and opened the curtains. Actors from eight towns in Croatia, three in Slovenia, and new actors from Duga Resa had never worked together. Yet what a miracle occurred on stage that the show went so well.

The next wave of children filled the hall at noon and loved the musical. At 6 p.m., we were back and ready for the adult performance. The final curtain dropped on a beautiful show, and the actors cheered. The day was long and exhausting but fulfilling.

The second and third days went well, filled with thousands of students by day and more adults by night. The public loved the show, but what blessed me was seeing the joy in my actors, all working on a common cause: love for the Lord and the arts.

Do we get tired of doing the same show over and over? I suppose. But for me, the joy is seeing people stream down the aisles to receive

Jesus. I never tire of seeing that. God's solution to bring actors together made this special.

After our three-day run, I was invited by the mayor of Duga Resa to lunch. The mayor was so impressed that a show of this caliber had come to his town that he wanted to invite me to come back and do another show anytime. What a nice compliment to get from a mayor. I hugged everyone goodbye and flew from Croatia to Moldova.

The Old Testament recounts numerous occasions when the Lord fought for His people—such as when the sun stood still for Joshua (Joshua 10:13). Or when God rained hail on Israel's enemies (Joshua 10:11). The Lord still fights on our behalf, especially when His Word needs to go forth.

My spiritual son and a friend, Pastor Alexander, had invited me to preach at an outdoor evangelistic event he was hosting in Chisinau, the capital. As I preached, a group from the Orthodox Church formed across the park and started yelling at us.

We tried to ignore them while I attempted to preach. I prayed and wondered what to say or do as I continued speaking. These Orthodox zealots meant to cause trouble, so they advanced on us, distracting and scaring the Christians in attendance.

Then something supernatural happened. An intense whirlwind appeared and blew between them and us, tossing over plastic chairs and sending trashcans and other debris into the air and raining down on them! Yet, none of it came near us. Right before our eyes, God intervened with a mini cyclone! It reminded me of His supernatural intervention between Pharaoh's army and the children of Israel. The religious fanatics were scared and ran away! The whirlwind stopped once they left, leaving us to finish our evangelistic event in peace. God's creative solution trumps anything we could've done.

Therefore, put on the full armor of God so that when the day of evil comes, you may be able to stand your ground, and after you have done everything, to stand.

—Ephesians 6:13

———— ◆◆ ————

By 2014, I was busier than ever, directing seven to eight theatrical productions with Cornerstone annually, plus an additional five shows on five continents with my friend Marc Accetta and *The View.*

Happily, most productions come and go with minimal stress. However, at least one production a year always tests my faith and determination.

In 2013, I was commissioned by the pastor's wife in Cape Town to write a musical on the life of Nelson Mandela. Honored by the request, I said yes. Over the year, I worked on writing the musical biography of this great man. I named the production *Madiba*—a Xhosa word that means "father"—the word every South African affectionately used when addressing Mr. Mandela.

I had done a comprehensive study on Mr. Mandela's life. In the script, I touched on all the milestones of his political life but avoided controversies. The musical begins with his upbringing as a prince of a Xhosa tribe whose father was the tribal king. The story follows his Christian upbringing and studies to become a lawyer, which led to his political activism and arrest, and his romantic affair with Winnie. She joined him in his work; they were arrested and later released from prison. The show finishes with his ascension to the presidency of South Africa. All this in two hours!

The manuscript was finished. I submitted the script to the church leadership. They loved it, and I had the green light to proceed. I started adding the music. The musical was inspirational, factual, and funny.

My focus is to bring people to Christ. I chose a perfect cast for the musical, and we went into production. Rehearsals were going well, but two weeks before we opened, the pastor's wife canceled the show.

Her reason? "We feel like it might be too controversial."

What? It's their history, and she was the one who commissioned the musical and later approved it. This show was far from controversial. Deeply saddened, I spoke to the cast, who were also heartbroken. I was careful, however, to present the situation in a way that they wouldn't harbor any resentment against their church leadership, as I'm mandated by God's Word to be a peacekeeper.

My friends in Port Elizabeth, pastors, and leaders caught wind of the situation. Unfazed by the change of heart in Cape Town, they expressed interest in the project. They knew me and knew the show would be a blessing. My bruised ego needed that healing balm.

I flew to Port Elizabeth, where my friend and assistant, Wendy, met me. She took me to Georgiou Spa, where I would be staying.

Auditions were scheduled, and I was able to cast the show with great actors and singers—including two incredible artists to play the roles of Nelson and Winnie Mandela.

Madiba is staged with many singing, dancing, and acting scenes with riots, fighting, chaos, and protests. Although this is part of South Africa's history, the scenes and subject can be disturbing if not carefully directed. I made the riots and the chaos as artistic as possible and choreographed the unrest to tell the story without offending anyone. The arrest scenes had lots of action. Four police, seven men, ran around the stage, fighting to music. I taught all the guys their choreographed fights and arrests, and they loved it.

Promotions began. Posters and banners went up all around the city, followed by television, radio, and newspaper interviews. The show drew lots of public attention due to its content of their national hero.

The day of the show had arrived. I was overwhelmed with the myriad of tasks still looming over us at these last moments before the show, but we pushed through.

I was still in my *Madiba* t-shirt and jeans behind the curtain when we opened the house to the public. I was nervous about the world premiere of my musical and the story of South Africa's national hero. No one had ever seen this show. What would the audience think? How would they respond? I've written many plays in the US, but I know US audiences. I didn't know South African audiences as well, and that troubled me. *What if the wife of the pastor in Cape Town was right?*

Backstage, I gave final notes and prayed with the actors as the audience filled the Opera House.

The majestic overture heralded through the auditorium announcing a historic moment as the title *Madiba* was emblazoned in light on the curtain. The tears welled in my eyes. I had struggled for a year and a half to come to this moment. Is this the joy a father feels when watching his baby being born?

I gave the command for the curtain to rise to a stage filled with White actors wearing crème and pastel colors, sitting under a gazebo sipping tea, frozen in a pose, drenched in dramatic lighting, creating a stunning tableau from another era. It looked like a photo taken from the Victorian era. In contrast, the Black actors wore bold primary colors in an African style creating a striking and colorful variation between the Whites and the Blacks as we opened with a musical dance number establishing Apartheid. In each following scene, the costumes, the sets, and the lighting accentuated a particular mood, and the dances and music were spellbinding. It was a work of art, and the audience was in amazement.

We ended with Mandela ascending to the presidency amidst a joyous and victorious celebratory dance from all of the chorus. We finished strong, and the audience gave us a standing ovation for what seemed hours. The cast was beside themselves with joy. We finished! The musical had finally opened. I thought of Cape Town, and I was saddened that the city was robbed of this blessing because of one person. How they would've loved this production. My Cape Town actors wrote and congratulated us.

The next day, I checked the reviews in the papers. The media reviews were positive, with the newspaper articles detailing each scene and giving glowing reports of the principal actors. The whole city was talking positively about our musical.

The third and final performance wasn't sad but joyous. The actors were determined to make this last performance the best yet. Audience members had read the reviews, so they filled the theatre. We had a lively crowd, and they loved the show. It went even better than the previous two performances. We finished strong. We took cast and crew photos, then had a cast party to celebrate a fantastic show. I love my actors.

The next day I went to the airport with some of my actors who wanted to see me off. I hugged them goodbye and flew off into the South African sunset.

Directing — South Korea

THE WAR BETWEEN LIGHT AND DARKNESS

The following year, I accepted another invitation to do a show in Port Elizabeth, South Africa. My assistant and dear friend, Wendy Pearce, picked me up and took me to this up-and-coming new church. The pastor had heard about all the previous shows I had done in PE and was excited about having a theatre project for his church. The kingdom of God had opened the door here in PE after many years. He offered to do the production in his church and to personally participate in it. That was great since we had neither the actors nor a venue. His stage was big enough for a musical and in a good location.

We held two nights of auditions for *Joseph* in his church and found a wealth of talent. The pastor's excitement was so infectious that all his church members were excited too. This is a huge church. We cast the show and had our first rehearsals.

Then, something strange happened the following week. For some unknown reason, the pastor decided that he didn't want us to use his church. He suggested we find a new hall. We obeyed, as he must have a good reason why he didn't want the show. We searched the city, as he asked, but couldn't find one. He simply shrugged it off and advised us to cancel the show altogether.

What? Why would he give up so quickly?

"Let me keep looking," I said. "Give me at least twenty-four hours."

He looked doubtful. "I'll give you until four thirty today." That was alarming.

With Wendy's help, we found a school with a beautiful theatre that'd charge us 80,000 rand ($5,000). We reserved the school's theatre and told the pastor.

"I don't think we can afford it," he said. "So the answer is still no." The kingdom of darkness was pushing the door shut.

Why the change of heart? He was so gung ho last week when I arrived, and now that we had a new cast who was excited, I had to question him.

"We don't have the 80,000 rand for the show," he explained.

Having strong faith and knowing how God provided many times for me in the past, I tried to assure him. "God will provide."

He laughed.

I challenged him.

"Give me twenty-four hours to find the money." He reluctantly agreed.

I spoke with my friends Philip and Yvette about the situation.

"We'd be happy to donate 40,000 rand for your show," they said. Then added, "Our son has something he wants to tell you." They handed the phone to their ten-year-old boy.

"Hi, Mr. Richard. I would like to donate my savings of 8000 rand to your show too."

Wow—I was so moved by their love offering. There was no hesitancy on their part. I thanked them very much and told them it was a great start. I could personally give 12,000 rand of my own money, so we had 60,000 rand (about $4,000). Surely this large church could provide the remaining 20,000 rand ($1000)? The kingdom of light was pushing the door back open.

The following day, I went to the church with the good news. I was ushered into a staff meeting, so I was excited to share with everyone. I told them all that had happened and how God had provided. Yet the reaction of everyone in the room baffled me. The staff didn't seem to know what to say, so they looked to their pastor for an answer.

"It's not possible," he said.

"Not possible?" I questioned. "But you said yesterday that you'd do the show if we could get a venue. I found one. Then you said if we could get the money, you'd do it. We have all but 20,000 rand, but God will provide that too. We only need half of the funds to sign the contract, 40,000 rand, and we currently have 60,000 rand. The other half is due at the performance five weeks from now. We've fulfilled all your conditions. We can do this now if you're still willing to help."

The pastor stood and looked coldly at me. "Sorry," then turned and walked out—just like that.

He left me sitting there with his staff, embarrassed. My face flushed red. They felt terrible for me but were torn between doing what was right or keeping their job. They all chose their job and reluctantly followed the pastor out, apologizing quietly to me as they left, leaving me sitting in their church's conference room alone. I could feel my face red, flustered, and half-angry. Had the kingdom of darkness won?

I closed my eyes and sighed. "Lord, if this is not Your will, I'll stop immediately."

But I felt Him quietly encourage me, "Go on."

I've never been one to give up. Determined, I shook it off and left. As I pulled out of the church parking lot, I got a call from another successful Christian businessperson from Port Elizabeth, who said he'd give 20,000 rand.

I couldn't believe it. We had all 80,000, just as I had told the pastor, but that didn't matter now. The pastor burned his bridge, and I didn't want to talk to him anymore. We had a perfect hall. Then I received one more surprise. After discovering we were a Christian organization doing a Christian musical, the school changed its mind on the price and felt they should let us have the hall for free. The kingdom of light was shining bright!

Right before my eyes, God was providing solution after solution. If only we had a pastor with enough faith. I have always said that you will succeed in God's kingdom if you will simply not give up. I told the actors the good news, and they were thrilled but embarrassed for their church. Rehearsals resumed at another church that Wendy had arranged for us, and we moved forward.

God came through on everything, including the use of other churches in the vicinity. We didn't have the costumes, but I had a solution—we'd borrow the ready-made costumes from Croatia.

I contacted two of my Croatian actresses, Iva and Blaža, for their help in bringing the costumes, and they were ecstatic to come. We'd pay for their tickets with the 80,000 rand we had leftover after the school graciously gave us the hall. The girls would bring the cases of costumes to South Africa. The week of the show was upon us. Iva and Blaža arrived with the costumes; we moved into the hall and set up platforms and sets.

The kingdom of darkness had tried to stop this production, yet we made it to the day of the show. But the devil and his kingdom weren't giving up quite yet.

I gave my workers marching orders that morning to work on the sets while I worked with the lighting and sound crew. At noon, a strange thing happened outside. Gale force winds began to blow. The winds were so strong that outdoor furniture blew away, and bushes and small trees were pulled out of the ground. It seemed indicative of a battle in the spiritual realm. This destructive show of power from the enemy had been intimidating from the beginning, trying to discourage us. Yet, we remained resolute, for I had seen our Lord do miracles before. The windows and doors rattled, and we were fearful. So I gathered the actors together, and we prayed that the wind would stop.

At four o'clock, the winds slowed to a mild breeze. At six o'clock, one hour before the show, the wind stopped. God had heard our prayer! Or so we thought. The enemy struck again, this time harder—the power went out in the city. It was pitch black, but I encouraged the workers to carry on. They used the lights from their cell phones and finished decorating.

While we worked, we sang songs of praise and worship. At seven o'clock, we seated the public. The kingdom of darkness had manifested itself in the dark hall. I was determined to let God have the victory if I simply chose not to give up. Fifteen minutes after we should've begun, there was still no power, and the public started getting restless, wanting to leave. I was at a loss for what to do. I announced that the children's choir would sing a few songs from the show, albeit in the dark. As they sang, I prayed earnestly for light. The audience was delighted and responded by giving them a huge ovation. Then an audience member told me he had two battery-powered floodlights in his truck and set them up. They provided great light.

With these lights on stands, I prepped the actors with a new idea: We would perform excerpts from the show. We would make the best of a bad situation while waiting for the electricity to come back on.

The crowd was surprised when we told them we'd continue. What a show!

There was a war in the spiritual realm. The enemy didn't want this show to happen, but God wanted to show us that His kingdom could not be stopped. The Holy Spirit was moving, and the devil was losing... *fast.*

The lights in the building never came on, but we had alternative lights, and we ended up performing our show a cappella with no microphones and no sound. The audience loved it more than if we had all the special sound effects. They understood the situation and what we were up against, and they cheered us on. Our show was spontaneous, simple, and from the heart. God was glorified. The kingdom of light had won!

After the show, everyone congratulated us for our spontaneity. I announced that they would have free entrance to a special matinee performance the following day created just for them since the evening show was already sold out.

The next day at noon, the actors arrived excited. Last night's impromptu performance turned out to be a blessing for the actors and me. It helped them to loosen up and relax in their roles. We started with a matinee performance at two o'clock. Surprisingly, the hall was nearly full with many who had attended the night before, who told others about the miracle performance.

The show went great, and the public loved it. We set up for the evening performance. We had a packed house, many coming from the church that had rejected us earlier, who showed up to encourage us. Judging by their thunderous ovation, we had a hit on our hands.

Sometimes your biggest challenge will turn out to be your biggest blessing. My secret? Go to God with your problem, and He will be faithful to provide you with a solution. And then, never give up!

After paying everyone for lights, sound, and other expenses, we had 20,000 rand left. But there was still one more vendor we needed to pay 27,000 rand, and she was there to collect. I went to her with the 20,000 and told her that's all we had for now, but we'd pay her the other 7,000 as soon as possible. She took the 20,000, waved the bills in front of me, and with a smile, said, "I saw your lovely show. If 20,000 rand is all you have, then that's all you owe me. Keep the 7,000 rand."

What a surprise. What a blessing, and what a saint. I couldn't thank her enough. We broke even, and we were finished.

The next day Philip and Yvette had their chauffeur drive me to the airport. I thought about the last few days. There had been a spiritual war. The devil and the kingdom of darkness did all they could to keep the show from happening. The situation seemed impossible, but God always had a solution. The kingdom of light had prevailed.

For God, who said, "Let light shine out of darkness," made his light shine in our hearts to give us the light of the knowledge of God's glory displayed in the face of Christ.
—2 Corinthians 4:6

———◆◆———

I went from one southern continent to another, from South Africa to South America. I had a friend who had been asking for a show in her native country of Colombia and had put me in contact with her pastor there. Of course, I was excited about going to Cartagena. The only thing is that the pastor isn't in this beautiful touristic city; he's in a tiny seaside village nearby called La Boquilla.

My hotel in La Boquilla was exactly fifty feet from the Pacific Ocean. Palm trees, sandy beaches, and a tiny village. It sounds like a dream! It was more of a nightmare.

In such a lazy little village, it's easy to find lazy pastors. We had twelve churches interested, but when it came to organizing, they quickly dropped out. They didn't want the show mainly because it was a lot of work. We began with twelve and ended with five pastors. I assured the five pastors that I'd do most of the work, but they remained negative.

On Sunday, I attended the five church services to promote the show. Each of the pastors talked about changing the world.

They preached, "It's faith and boldness that will allow us to take all of Colombia and the world for Christ!" followed by applause and a chorus of amens.

Yet, the next day, these same fearless preachers for Christ doubted how we could do such a show in this tiny village. I encouraged them that God would provide, and they needn't worry. But they did, and two more pastors dropped out. I was tired of encouraging them. They didn't want the show, so why must I stay? Cartagena had more prominent churches, and they were more likely to do a big show. These pastors were a lost cause.

I came to my hotel, bent on canceling the show. However, like before, I felt the Lord's voice, but it wasn't gentle this time. It was the voice of a father correcting his son:

"Where did I send you?"

"La Boquilla."

"Then why are you trying to make a show in Cartagena?"

"Lord, the pastors here are…"

"I didn't ask you about the pastors."

"But I'm so frustrated because they are…"

"I didn't ask how you feel."

He asked again, "Where did I send you to do the show?"

"La Boquilla"

And that was it. I get it now. Cartagena is modern and clean. La Boquilla is a collection of homeless, drug-addicted prostitutes, uneducated thieves, and just downright poor people. Who needs Jesus more than these people do? I asked for God's forgiveness. God wanted me to love the *least* of these unconditionally.

I got to work and met some amazing people who helped us find a place to perform. There were no halls in this village, so we rented the football field in the center of La Boquilla. It had stadium lights at night that could be used for our performance. It had bars and discos surrounding the football field that blared their music as loud as possible. Over the weeks, I went to each owner and asked them if they could please not play any music from 7 to 10 p.m. on the one night of our event while we did our evangelistic outreach. Hispanics are religious by nature, so they agreed to do so for one night during the performance.

Through the help of church friends, we found stage platforms, set builders, and a Christian man who would rent us sound and lights. He also had smoke machines, strobes, and a generator. I wasn't excited about the generator, mainly due to the price. It doubled our price. I reasoned we could plug the lights right into the football field where we would do the show. However, the Lord reminded me of our recent show in South Africa, so I rented the generator.

We had cast almost all the roles, but I didn't have an actor with a good voice for the role of the voice of God. I could only think of one, Alejandro Sarmiento, who had done the role many years earlier in the USA. Since I was paying for everything for the show, I had almost no funds to offer him for his airline ticket.

I called him. "Alejandro? Hello. It's Richard calling from Colombia. I need you to come and do the role of the Voice of God for the production here."

"Hi, Richard! It's been many years. When is the show?"

"Next week. Can you get off work and come for five days?"

Silence.

I kept speaking, "Oh, and I have no money. Can you pay for the airfare yourself?"

Silence.

Finally, he responded, "I'll have to pray about it."

"Thanks, Alejandro. Let me know as soon as possible. God bless you." *Click.*

I didn't doubt God. I had too much to think about, so I left that with the Lord. The next day, I got a confirmation from Alejandro that he could come from the US to help us with the show! And he'd pay for his own ticket! Thank You, Lord!

It was the day before the show, and I went to the airport in Cartagena to pick God up. I was so happy to see him. We worked with the actors, and they all loved Alejandro's voice.

The next day was opening day, and I had been given the assurance that the men were putting up the stage and building the platforms. Lights and sound were going up, and we had rented one thousand white plastic chairs, so I was happy everything was under control, so I worked with the actors.

The next day, I went with Alejandro to the football field, expecting to see the seats lined orderly into rows and the platform and towers up. Instead, what I saw was a disaster! I expected to see the sets up, the walls covered, and the columns up. No, nothing, not even the chairs were in place but were in high stacks where the truck must've just dumped them and left. We had so much work to do, and it was 5:30 p.m. I went into director mode and started giving commands.

I even put Alejandro and others to put out chairs. I worked with the guys, showing them how to cover the stairs, the walls, heaven, mount the columns, and cover the Book of Life. Good heavens! Lighting was there but was woefully inadequate. I had ordered thirty lights, but there were only four on the stage and four hanging! A total of eight.

Oh Lord, help me not to kill the lighting guys.

The lighting team was a couple of eighteen-year-olds who had no clue what they were doing. Only the sound guy seemed to be the closest thing to a professional. It was now 7 p.m., time to begin, and we weren't close to being ready. Still, it didn't matter because only around forty to fifty people had arrived in a sea of 1000 chairs. I was discouraged. The lighting wasn't prepared or connected, so I pushed them. I had a war with a worker with the smoke machines, which were placed poorly, meaning the actors would trip over them if left where the light man wanted them.

At 8 p.m., I went to see the progress on the lights but saw that nothing was done. I found the workers in their truck, eating! I took the food boxes away from them and said, "Do you see these people? They're waiting for a show, and I can't begin until you guys finish your lights!" They were mad. I was furious. Since I hadn't paid them yet, I held leverage over them. They finally finished, but it was now 8:30 p.m. We began one point five hours late.

Still, the worst was yet to come. I had asked all the bars surrounding the sports field to promise not to play their blaring music between seven to ten pm just this one night, and they all agreed. But now? The music was blasting louder than ever. We could hear the actors because of the microphones, but the distraction from the loud music was a huge problem. We had begun the first scene. I prayed, "Lord, what more can I do? Please do a miracle so that we can reach the people." The Lord said, "Son, I want these people saved more than you do." That calmed me down as I let that soak deep into my spirit.

We had reached the time in the show when we would hear the voice of God talk. Suddenly, boom! All the power in the town went out. All of it! It was pitch black and eerily silent. No blaring music, no disco lights, nothing. It was a sea of darkness and stillness. Except for us! We had a generator, so we were the only ones in town who had power, lights, sound, and music. No one else did. Suddenly, a lone voice boomed through the dark night sky: the voice of God. It was chilling!

The people started to arrive. (Since they couldn't stay in the dark. People are attracted to light.) Since we were the only thing going, people continued to arrive… thousands. The crowd found the drama amazing and beautiful. They laughed and cried. And still, the people kept coming. God's kingdom of light was gleaming brightly in the sea of darkness. The people loved the show.

We had over 4000 people by the end of the show, and at the altar call, 1000 people came forward for salvation! Wow! Thank You, Lord. The actors were thrilled, the audience was thrilled, and I was in awe of God's miraculous move to save His performance. He had commanded me to stay, not just to be drowned out by the kingdom of darkness.

We took cast pictures afterward, and we took the sets down. The pastors from the city came and were amazed at God's ability to take charge. He saved us. God wanted to teach these pastors that He responds to faith and prayer, and now He would make sure this show was fruitful. The next day, I said goodbye to Alejandro and the rest of my actors and flew out of Colombia.

Kyiv, Ukraine

STORIES
FROM THE
MISSION FIELD

It had been invited to come and do a production in Davao City, Philippines. Ken, a friend from Christ for the Nations, worked as a lifelong missionary there. We prepared for the production, and I saw a lot of talent. Filipinos are passionate about the arts. It turns out they're also passionate about life.

We had printed tickets, but they were more for promotions, meaning they could use them at any of the four performances at the 2000-seat auditorium.

On opening day, we weren't expecting what would happen. We opened the hall, and the people came running in, flooding the performance hall. This happened for all four evenings of the performances.

It was exciting to see so much enthusiasm until the hall filled for the final night. As it looked like we would be full, security closed the doors to the building allowing those who had entered to remain in the lobby. We were full, but outside the building, there were still thousands waiting to enter. They were mad because they said they had a ticket. Knowing it was the last performance, people started pushing on the windows and the glass doors with metal frames. They weakened them so much that we were afraid that they would destroy this property as they rioted.

Ken quickly spoke with the theatre manager, who, seeing the situation, allowed us an extra performance for the following night. They both then went outside to calm the unruly crowd. A promise was made to those outside that a special performance would be presented the following evening. This helped quell the masses, and they left, allowing us to do our production.

The performances finished well, and at the altar call, we had thousands come forward for salvation! Best of all, because of this experience, many of the actors are in full-time ministry today. Filipinos are kind by nature, and their heart for the things of God is inspiring. However, from this experience, I learned to print a specific number of tickets for each performance, even with a free admission. It's an easier way to control a crowd.

While I prepared for the show in Davao City, Philippines, I was invited to minister to the Badjaos people in the southern region of Mindanao. What makes these people so unique is that they live in bamboo huts on stilts over the Davao Gulf. The people connect their huts by securing a single, long plank of coconut lumber between each hut high above the water below.

As we arrived at the village, I was surprised to see that the huts had no windows, no doors, as the stifling heat didn't allow you to be enclosed. There were no beds or chairs. The people sat on the floor. Each home had a hole in the corner of the house, which served as the toilet.

The shocking part for me was that they fished, bathed, and washed clothes in this same water. A family had invited me to dinner, and as I watched, the father dove from the house into the water thirty feet (ten meters) below and caught a fish within seconds! Impressive! But I passed on the entree. I ate the fruit and vegetables instead.

Due to the salty and polluted water where they live, the people have to carry by hand large jugs of fresh water or create a primitive water aqueduct from large bamboo tubes elevated by coconut lumber. The water is used and reused, making it unsanitary.

Later, as I preached in the church in their area, people came forward for prayer. A father carried his six-year-old son in and laid him before me, heartbroken. He cried, "My son is so sick. Can you pray that God would heal him?" The child had dysentery from the water. I prayed for him, of course, but what these people needed was a reliable and sanitary supply of fresh water. Lord, help them.

———————◆◆◆———————

Ken's wife took a small group to evangelize some cannibals named the Ubo tribe. It's hard to imagine that in the twenty-first century, cannibalism still exists, but it does. The tribe lives on Mindanao island in the Cotabato province, several hours from Davao City by vehicle, followed by a half-day mountain hike on foot to reach their territory. I asked if I could go. This had to be a special moment! Yet, I wasn't allowed to go, so I wondered why. They said, "You are tall, and therefore you are not safe."

I later interviewed a former cannibal who was now born again. He told me that a cannibal doesn't eat people for food. Rather, they believe that the traits of a person reside in the liver, kidneys, or other specific organs. If a cannibal finds something attractive about another person, they distract the person, hit them over the head, then eat the vital organs to obtain the other person's traits. They then bury the rest of the body. I asked him if he'd eaten anyone before he was born again. He said with the most radiant smile, "Of course."

It was Easter time in Kyiv, Ukraine, and I was there to direct a beautiful musical to celebrate the resurrection of Jesus. We went straight into auditions, announced the new cast, handed out their scripts, and geared up for our Easter musical.

I found out that my costumer from the USA, Amy Harriss, would be coming with her fantastic costumes. She arrived and got to work, sewing and altering costumes to fit each actor.

The cast was wonderful, except for one. The actor playing the role of Jesus was gorgeous. Vladimir was the most handsome Jesus I'd ever cast. He was tall and athletic, with gloriously long, naturally auburn hair and a full, well-trimmed beard. He looked amazing. The problem was… he knew it.

He argued with me for weeks about changing his lines and staging. He had very definite ideas of how Jesus should act.

"Richard, I shouldn't have to cross the stage to wash their feet," he waved a finger at the disciples.

"I should be standing here, and they should come to me."

"I don't want my lines to be Scripture. I want to use my own words."

I'd had my fill of his spoiled defiance and put my foot down.

"Vlad, how many shows have you ever directed?"

"None."

"How many times have you been in a theatrical production?"

He rolled his eyes. "None."

"I've directed over 500 productions in a hundred countries, Vlad, so maybe, I have a little more experience in knowing what works and what doesn't. So please do what I ask, like every other actor, or I will be forced to find someone else to play your role."

Vlad's face went slack. He pondered my ultimatum.

"Okay!" He threw his arms up in the air. "We'll do it your way."

I wish that conversation would have been the end of it. The following week, as we staged the crucifixion scene, we needed to practice putting him on the cross so that he would be secure of what to do on the cross during the show. I always think about safety first, but that didn't matter to him. I let the centurions raise the cross alone so that they'd know how to work together to maneuver the cross into a vertical position and insert it into the reinforced hole. They did it with no problem. Next, we lifted one of the workers on the cross to show Vlad how safe it was. It was easy. Now, it was time for Vlad to practice. He reacted like a child.

"No! I don't want to. I might fall. I'm scared."

"Vlad," I reasoned, "it's safe, complete with handles you can hold, see?" Even I got on the cross, and the centurions lifted me. "See? Please, get on the cross."

He refused. "What kind of an irresponsible director puts the lives of his actors in danger? I could fall."

I felt my face get hot with anger.

After pleading patiently with a petulant child, I finally demanded, "Vlad, just get on the cross! I have been doing this show for thirty years, with multiple actors in multiple countries, all in this role. We have never had anyone fall. Why would you think we would put you in danger? Now, get on that cross!"

How embarrassing. This was all done in front of the cast and crew. Reluctantly, he eased himself onto the cross. To get him acclimatized to the process, we lifted him three times. Each time, safely. No matter, he still complained to anyone within earshot. Every time! He also didn't want to be taken down off the cross, so here we went again! He finally did all we needed him to do, but I never knew I could get so mad with Jesus!

During the performances, he wanted more time to change into resurrected Jesus. Thankfully, Amy was backstage to help Vlad go from bloody Jesus to glorified Jesus, complete with a harness connecting him to cables to lift, all within three minutes; otherwise, he would've never made it. Vlad wanted to fluff his hair and look in a mirror, but he came out of the tomb with Amy pushing him out on cue! The public wasn't aware of all this. They only saw Jesus gloriously come out of the tomb, but the real show was backstage!

On another performance of an Easter musical, the show was going well. The actors performed a near-perfect performance. Until, that is, the majestic musical introduction began for Pilate's grand entrance. The actor playing the role of Pilate was to make his entrance, but he didn't appear. Backstage, my heart started pounding backstage.

We waited for a beat, then played Pilate's musical entrance again. No Pilate. Jesus, the centurions, the Pharisees, and a beautiful Roman set with a majestic governor's throne center stage were all in position. Except Pilate. You can't crucify Jesus without Pilate! I was on the radio telling everyone to find him. Cast and crew were running behind the curtain looking for Pilate, but no one could find him. At a loss of what to do, we tried to get Caiaphas to ad-lib, but nothing. Again, we played his intro music. Still no Pilate!

I was frantic. Where was Pilate? I prayed a desperate prayer, and we cued his entrance once more. Finally, out of nowhere, Pilate came running out. Not exactly the majestic entrance the script calls for. He had been outside the building reviewing his lines. Actors!

And people wonder why I have gray hair.

In Nicaragua, I had lunch with Pastor Jorge, a friend who's the director of all the Assembly of God churches in the area. He had participated in an earlier theatrical production.

Pastor Jorge said, "This show was a dream come true for me."

I cocked my head. "I haven't had many pastors say that. Why is that?"

He explained, "When I was a boy, my father had found an evangelistic drama on video that impacted him so much. He started a small ministry, sharing the video with other church congregations.

"I was ten at the time, and I followed my father to these churches and helped set up his projector, the screen, and chairs. You can't imagine how many times I have seen this drama.

"Ever since, I've dreamed of acting in a professional drama like what I saw on that video. So, when I heard that you were a professional director wanting to do a musical here, I naturally had this tremendous urge to be a part, so I auditioned."

His story was precious. I would, of course, cast him. But I had an obvious question.

"Pastor Jorge, you've got me curious. I'd like to see the video that inspired you. What was the video you and your father showed all those years?"

"*El Trono del Juicio. The Judgment Seat.* It was videoed in the USA."

"*El Trono del Juicio?*" I asked, startled by the discovery. "Jorge, that's the show I directed!"

He said, "No, this was directed in the USA."

I said, "I know! That was my church we videoed the show in!" We were both surprised by the coincidence.

Wow, what a fantastic blessing! You never know when or how you are influencing a person's life. A show from thirty years ago is still touching lives today!

THE
STATE OF
FEAR

The year 2020. Does anything else need to be said? I think everyone remembers what happened before and after that fateful day on March 15 when the world changed forever into a bizarre episode of *The Twilight Zone*. Me? I approached the year 2020, confident this would be a great year. Hindsight, however, is always twenty-twenty.

I was ministering in Guatemala as the year began, organizing another musical production of *Joseph the Dreamer* with Pastor Rony Madrid at Vida Real Church in Guatemala City. A modern church in every way, the congregation is home to many young talented people excited to participate in a grand musical. I was eager to begin and anticipated the public opening on March 13.

The church spared no expense for the sets, costumes, and theatre curtains. The whole look and feel of the theatre and presentation were professionally organized, just the way I wish every production would be. Having never seen a Christian presentation like this before, the public was amazed as we swept them away into the land of Egypt as described in the book of Genesis. They clapped. They cheered. But most importantly, they came forward to know more about our Lord, Jesus. The production proceeded beautifully, sending my soul soaring until…

"Richard, I need to talk with you," the pastor whispered to me behind the curtain on the second night. "We have to cancel the run."

My hands got sweaty, and my heart raced as his words sunk in. He then repeated his announcement to the audience. We wouldn't be able to do the final performance.

I immediately went into "strike mode," a theatre term for dismantling the stage, packing the costumes, taking cast pictures, and saying goodbye. While everyone carried out their strike orders, my mind raced. *COVID. What's COVID?*

When I prepare a show, I'm deeply involved in the day-to-day production challenges leading up to the opening night. I was in my bubble, so I knew nothing about this new malady.

With the show canceled, I figured I'd fly home the next day. I arrived at La Aurora International airport in Guatemala City. A mass of people stood outside the building. I thought there had been a bomb threat inside. I went to the security at the front door.

"You can't come in." The guard shook his head and pointed back to the parking lot.

I countered, "But I must enter. I have a flight in two hours."

"Not today—you don't. Maybe another day."

I tried to understand. "When can I fly?"

"Two, three days. Maybe a week. Now please, you must go." He gestured again to the parking area.

What was I going to do in Guatemala for another seven days? *I have a busy schedule!*

I lived in a beautiful blue villa. A one-story house with a courtyard surrounded by plants and flowers and an orange tree covered with oranges. Around the courtyard were twelve-foot (four meters) concrete walls with barbed wire coiled around the top. A heavy iron door guarded the courtyard, and iron bars protected every window. Most banks weren't as securely guarded as I was.

I had become friends with the owners, and they let me extend my stay another seven days.

Seven days stretched into seven months! With so much time on my hands, I decided to write a new musical, plus translate the entire musical of *The Promise* into Spanish, including the songs.

In September, I was finally a free man and allowed to fly home to Dallas. The journey to the States was eerie—an empty Guatemalan airport, an empty plane, and an empty Dallas airport. I was back at work as part of the team on a virtual show of *The View* with my friend, Marc Accetta. We filmed in a studio in North Dallas.

Despite the travel restrictions and warnings about this new virus, I felt led to continue my international ministry. I refused to be controlled by fear, but rather, I'm led by the Holy Spirit, and the Spirit was leading me to Nicaragua in late October to begin production on a Christmas show.

We presented a beautiful Christmas musical as a gift to the precious citizens of Managua in celebration of the birth of Jesus. We finished this year as we began with a beautiful show, but I knew life across the globe would never be the same.

Around the world, people welcomed the new year with a chorus of prayers. Everyone everywhere was happy to see 2020 behind us as we hoped for a better 2021.

Travel restrictions continued to complicate my international ministry. I was still in Nicaragua and had no other invitation for the year. They wanted another show, so I prepared for our Easter show. The months I'd been sequestered in Guatemala translating *The Promise* into Spanish finally bore fruit. We brought the musical life of Jesus from the script to the stage in Spanish! We booked the National Theatre Rubén Darío and got to work. We would make all the costumes, backdrops, and sets from scratch. We had the time, and we wanted this show to be the biggest and best we'd ever done.

———◆◆———

I need to pause to speak of a talented Christian woman from Managua. Dina has a home business that she operates with her sister and mother. She took on the challenge of creating hundreds of our costumes for the show. This family is gifted in crafting costumes, but they also live in extreme poverty. Their house was falling apart. There was no window, just an opening with cardboard nailed to the top of the window to keep the wind and rain out. Their fence in front of their home was rotting and swaying in the wind.

Dina's father is paralyzed. In what seemed like a continuation of unfortunate circumstances, Dina suffered a stroke while constructing our costumes.

Paralyzed, she could no longer raise her left arm or left leg or speak. She needed to be tied to her chair to keep her from falling over. Dina's elderly mother and sister were left to care for the two disabled house members. This costume job was meant to be a financial godsend for them and beautiful costumes for us, but the devil saw an opportunity to destroy their blessings and ours. The project came to a standstill.

I was on a tight schedule to finish the costumes, but this severe situation with Dina and her family couldn't be ignored. Dina needed medical attention fast, and the house needed serious repairs. These two situations were way beyond the finances and abilities of their random sewing projects.

> *Religion that God our Father accepts as pure and faultless is this: to look after orphans and widows in their distress and keep oneself from being polluted by the world.*
>
> —James 1:27

I had to act. I found a doctor specializing in stroke victims. I spoke with him and negotiated a deal to meet Dina's medical needs. Then, with the help of Jonathan, my faithful Nicaraguan assistant, we coordinated the materials needed to repair Dina's home. With the help of some hired builders Jonathan had found, we removed the falling fence and replaced it with a sturdy brick and iron fence and gate. The house's front wall was rebuilt, making way for windows and a door. Genuine working windows and a decorative front door that locked were professionally installed. To complete the newly remodeled home, we had the front garden and porch landscaped with bushes and flowers.

The look on the family's faces and the tears they shed when they saw their beautiful, remodeled home for the first time were priceless. But it gets better. In the time it took for the house to be rebuilt, Dina's body was also rebuilt. God was doing a miracle through her therapist, and she was back to normal, using all her limbs and voice. God not only restored her body but restored the family's hope in Him. The ladies finished off the costumes beautifully and on time for the show. I paid Dina and her sisters well for the beautiful costumes and prayed for God's continued blessings as we left them to enjoy the fruits of their labor and their new home.

———◆◆◆———

My costumer friend from Texas, Amy, had helped me with productions in South Korea, Ukraine, Mexico, and the USA. Now she was creating some of the more technically challenging costumes for our show in Nicaragua. The week of the show, she arrived with all her unique creations, dazzling the actors. With stunning sets and imaginative props being built, this musical would be one to remember.

In March, the show opened to a packed house at the National Theatre Rubén Darío. Night after night, the show's glorious music, talented actors, elegant costumes, and special effects blessed the public. The show came to a successful end for the year.

We took the sets down and put everything in storage. However, another church saw the show earlier and wanted to present the musical at the National Theatre again. This time, perform it for their large congregation. Of course, they'd pay for everything. But goodness! We had just taken everything down! We put the sets back up and performed two encores of the production to more packed houses in early April.

I had no other show on my calendar for 2021. I prayed, "Lord, thank You for two shows in Nicaragua. Here I am at Your call." I resigned myself to stay home, pray, and wait on God. The Lord answered quicker than I thought.

In April, I received a surprise email from Kyiv, Ukraine. "Richard, can you do a show with us for May?" Pastor Henry Madava inquired. "A show? Let me check my schedule," I bluffed. I waited one hour, then wrote him, "Give me two days, and I'll be on a plane to Kyiv." I had a show for May! The show went well and was an artistic and spiritual success. I thanked the Lord for a third show for the year.

In May, I got another invitation for June in Chernivtsi. I took a train from Kyiv, had the auditions and the rehearsals, and presented our show in June outside in a beautiful park with a great outdoor theatre. A fourth show.

In June, I got another invitation to Ivano Frankivsk from another pastor, and so we presented a beautiful show in July in the national theatre in the city. A fifth show.

In July, I received yet another invitation from pastors in Uzhgorod who had heard of my Ukrainian tour. I went there, and we presented our show in August. Surely, this would be all. I was grateful to God for a sixth show.

In August, I received yet one more invitation, this time outside of Ukraine. In Warsaw, Poland, I flew to present a show for September. Wow, a seventh show!

This seems all a bit repetitious. I agree. Yet, there is a reason why I mention these invitations individually. God's ways are far above man's ways. Not only were these miraculous invitations that were occurring independent of each other, but the Lord was also introducing me to many new churches that would be essential during the coming Ukrainian war.

The miracle invitations kept coming.

In September, we got the green light to proceed with the twenty-second annual production of *The View* with my friend, Marc Accetta. We would do our show in October in Las Vegas. An eighth show!

In October, my friend Pastor Juan Constantino arranged for me to come to Guatemala for a Christmas show in November and December. What a string of surprises as I left to begin my ninth show for the year!

———◆◆———

In November, I landed in Guatemala and arrived in the city of Chichicastenango, the capital of the Quiche region located in the country's highlands. Here is where the ancient Mayan people have continued to live over the centuries.

Due to the difficulty of reaching this region in the Chuacus mountains, the people aren't integrated with the rest of the country of Guatemala, so they cling to their ancient and unique Mayan history—a colorful past with an alarming custom of visiting witch doctors at the marketplace while shopping. An imposing active pagan altar can be found there, where animal and bird sacrifices are made daily by the city's witch doctor.

What I found unsettling about this ancient city was that a bomb exploded by day and by night every hour or two! I was informed of this strange custom: the Mayans believe the intentional explosions ward off demons and keep their town safe.

The Catholic Church hopes to change this pagan belief by teaching the Mayan people instead to take a statue of the apostle Thomas, the city's patron saint, and parade it from one house to another. The belief is that if the statue is brought to your home for one hour, you'll be blessed for the next year and be safe from demonic activity.

A priest leads the procession, followed by believers carrying the statue and an oompah band playing joyous Mayan Catholic songs. When the statue reaches the house, the residents celebrate by shooting bottle rockets into the sky and throwing firecrackers in the street, even at night.

With all this noise, it's hard to sleep. At three in the morning, you hear an explosion set off by those warding off demons, followed by the Catholic's *oompah-oompah*, then the whistle of the bottle rockets, and finally by the loud crackle of firecrackers. Nothing is boring about Chichicastenango.

By the end of my time there, I'd gotten used to the noise and even found some humor in it all, but I don't think I slept a whole night while I was there.

Our Christmas show with these Indigenous people went well. The actors, steeped in their Mayan culture, had no clue what a theatrical performance was. And now here they were, singing and dancing American dances wearing colorful glittering vests, and the audience loved it!

We finished our run, said goodbye to the precious Mayan Christians, and flew back to Dallas to spend Christmas with my family and friends. In reflection, I marveled at how the Lord had transformed my calendar from one show in the books to nine shows. He's a miracle-working God!

Managua, Nicaragua

HISTORY
REPEATS
ITSELF

I begin each new year with a prayer, "May this be the year of Your return. Come, Lord Jesus."

With this prayer, I began my thirty-fifth world tour. I was incredibly excited about this year. For the first time, I had a four-show lineup from January through May, all in my favorite country, Ukraine.

I landed in Kyiv on New Year's Eve to usher in the year with my Ukrainian friends, Kirill and Anton. The next day I reported for duty in Ivano Frankivsk, the same city I had done a show in last July. Ironically, Pastor Yuri and I agreed on a World War II drama, *The Hiding Place*. Who could imagine that the drama's plot would have such an uncanny similarity to what we were about to experience?

With a wonderful cast of actors, we began rehearsals in January. The actors had memorized their lines and staging by mid-February, and we tweaked the show as the scenery and the costumes were being created for our opening performances in the beginning of March. We noticed a distinct correlation between what we were rehearsing on stage and what we saw play out politically in real life.

The Hiding Place opens with a colorful scene where guests enjoy cake and coffee at the home of the ten Boom family as they celebrate an anniversary. The conversation turns to a serious topic as guests discuss the threat of imminent invasion by Hitler and his German army.

In real time, my friend, Kirill Dubovoy, was getting married on February 20. I was in Kyiv to participate in their beautiful and colorful wedding. At the reception filled with refreshments, we discussed the possible invasion by Putin and his Russian army.

In scene two of *The Hiding Place,* the ten Booms sit around the radio and listen to the prime minister reassure the country that there will be no war and that Hollanders must remain calm.

In real time, back in Ivano Frankivsk, we listened to television announcements assuring everyone that Putin was only holding military exercises along the border and Ukrainians needn't worry, so I didn't concern myself further with the news.

In scene three of *The Hiding Place*, war has broken out. Our protagonist, Corrie ten Boom, wakes to bombs exploding above her. War! She and her sister run downstairs, pray, and begin making plans.

In real time, on Thursday, February 24, I was startled awake at 6 a.m. by multiple explosions in Ivano Frankivsk. War! I've heard large bombs explode in the movies but never live in person. The windows rattled. The flat trembled. Pictures fell off the wall. Each explosion felt like a punch to the chest. The experience was terrifying! My thoughts went wild. Should I hide? Should I run? I dressed quickly and ran downstairs to see to what extent this trouble had escalated and found people outside were running frantically in all directions. I finally understood how serious the situation had become.

Knowing I would need cash, I ran to the nearest cash machine, but it was inoperable. A cyberattack the night before had rendered all banks and cash machines useless. I ran around the corner to the store, but the lines there stretched down the street, and the people inside were hoarding, so supplies wouldn't last. All bus tickets were sold out, and at the train station, hundreds were packing on the trains. I couldn't make it with all my blue luggage. A sickening feeling squeezed my stomach. I needed to flee the country, but where would I—where could I go?

Suddenly, I got a call from my assistant as if on cue. "There is a car leaving for Hungary right now. Be ready outside in twenty minutes!"

I never packed faster in my life. I ran to the meeting point, where I met one of my actors, Rostislav, and his wife, Yulia, who was seven months pregnant. That afternoon we drove several hours to the border. We were hungry and almost stopped for dinner but decided to cross into Hungary first. A long line of cars waited at the border. The wait would be hours long as cars slowly crept forward. Chaos and confusion reigned; the guards were inundated by Ukrainians escaping their country.

By a miracle, Yulia saw one of her girlfriends walking by our car. As Yulia asked what she was doing here, she said she was dating one of the border guards and was here visiting him. We asked the obvious question, and he told her he would help us and allowed us to go to the front of the line, where he processed our documents and let us cross the border leaving Ukraine.

We made it into Hungary!

We didn't know it at the time, but a miracle had just occurred. Forty minutes after we crossed the border, the guards closed the borders to all Ukrainian men eighteen to sixty years old; they were ordered to stay behind and fight alongside the small Ukrainian military. Women and children could flee, but the men were turned back. Rostislav is twenty-seven years old and made it out just in time to be with his pregnant wife.

In scene four in *The Hiding Place*, the German army invades and slowly takes over Holland. Although the media promised that civilians would not be attacked, days later, all Jewish people were targeted, arrested, and beaten while buildings were being destroyed.

In real time, the Russian army converged on Ukraine from three sides while we continued our trek northward from Hungary through Slovakia and into Poland. News circulated of Ukrainian schools and apartment buildings being blasted by tanks with civilians hurt or killed, to the shock and sadness of all Ukrainian citizens.

I met up with a dear friend and actor Piotr and his wife, Anna, who offered me a safe place and another flat for Rostislav and Yulia. I thanked Rostisalv profusely for his help in driving me out of Ukraine.

When Corrie ten Boom sees the chaos and damage in her country, she joins the Underground movement and houses the Jews fleeing the grip of the Nazis.

In real time, thousands were arriving from Ukraine into Poland, and I couldn't just sit around and do nothing. I wanted to help those fleeing their country, and I recognized some of the faces in the crowd. We were happy to see each other but imagine my shock to now see them as refugees. These are not nameless refugees to me. They're friends, former actors, and brothers and sisters in Christ. It's heart-breaking knowing how comfortable and secure their lives in Ukraine had been, and now they were far away from the homes they worked so hard for. They were in tents with no heat, under blankets, and in sleeping bags. They had no running water, no bathrooms, no internet, no food, money, or gas. Suddenly, they'd been lowered to the most basic of necessities—their dignity stripped, fleeing for their lives. These people and images flooded my mind, and I couldn't shake them loose. I must do something, but dear Lord, what?

I had directed a successful show with several Polish churches the previous September, so I contacted the pastors and coordinators who made thousands of sandwiches and provided hot drinks and aid to arriving refugees. They were willing to help but unsure of what to do as this was only day two of the war. I went into director mode and used my experience as a producer and director of shows to organize and activate the churches in Poland to help the refugees. They provided shelter, food, and other necessities beyond the abilities of these displaced people. My coordinator for the show back in September, Vadim, and the pastor who invited me, Pastor Oleksandr Demianenko, were both vital instruments to house, clothe, and feed untold numbers of refugees.

The refugees continued to pour into Poland, and I was at a loss of where to send them. Suddenly it hit me: Summer camps! Across Poland, camp facilities sat empty during winter. I contacted one; they could accommodate 300 people. As we started to move people there, we got a phone call that the orphans from Ukraine were being evacuated and were coming in six busses filled with 300 children. The dilemma was that the only available shelter was for twenty children in one school, thirty in one church, etc. They had limited orphan parents and hoped for one place for all of them, but where? The Lord's amazing word earlier provided the solution: The summer camp! The orphans were thrilled to have a place where they could all stay together.

I posted on Facebook what I was experiencing in Poland beyond the Ukrainian border. Around the world, people watched the story unfold, and here I was in the middle of it all. To my surprise, my post generated so much interest. Christian friends from around the world asked where they could give and how they could help. I posted links to various churches in Ukraine and Poland to help the refugees, and people responded. I funneled the funds to churches in Ukraine assisting those affected by the war, as well as funds to churches in Poland, Croatia, and beyond.

In *The Hiding Place*, Corrie ten Boom's father, Caspar, is threatened by a Nazi who tells him, "I'm going to arrest you. But I'll let you stay in your house if you promise not to help any more Jews. Agreed?"

"If I stay home," Papa ten Boom replies, "I will open my door to anyone in need."

In real time, Ukrainians continued to make their way to western Europe. I was determined to stay and help as many as possible for as long as possible.

Over the next six weeks, I moved to Croatia and found lodging for refugees migrating westward. I organized churches where I had done shows in Poland, Croatia, Spain, Great Britain, Italy, the Netherlands, and Germany. My actor Danijel Behin and his sweet wife, Gris, a wonderful young couple, worked tirelessly to serve over 1000 refugees. This is what superheroes look like. We established transportation logistics through local churches. We had trucks filled with food delivered to the churches. We recruited church volunteers to distribute groceries, bedding, linens, and clothes. The churches did such a phenomenal job and took the reins that I worked myself out of a job!

My body was weary, and my mind was thick with troubled thoughts trying to find solutions for too many refugees. By night, sleep became difficult, my dreams laced with exploding bombs and overwhelmed with people everywhere needing help. By day, I found myself running from Germany to the Netherlands as the Ukrainian refugees slowly migrated throughout Europe and beyond, needing my help and my contacts.

Since I've performed many shows in Russia and Ukraine for many years, people ask, "Who are you for, Russia or Ukraine?" My response is that I'm for the more than five million displaced refugees who have been tragically affected by this war. I pray for peace. I pray for justice.

I pray for the souls of both Russians and Ukrainians, and most of all, I pray for our Lord's swift return.

"May this be the year of Your return. Come, Lord Jesus."

My time in Croatia was up, as I had a theatrical production lined up for June after my last show in Ukraine in May, which of course, never materialized.

I flew to the US and enjoyed the peace and quiet of a world far away from conflict and the struggles plaguing Europe as this war raged.

In May, I flew to Yerevan, Armenia, country number 101! Towering over the city, evident to all, is the majestic Mount Ararat, where Noah's ark landed millennia ago. According to the pastors here, Noah descended from Mount Ararat and into Yerevan. So humanity began again here in Armenia. From here, some of Noah's descendants, namely Shem and his descendants, headed due south about 800 miles (1300 km). That's where you find Ur (in modern-day Iraq). From there, Terah, Abraham's father, headed northwest for Haran (in modern-day Turkey), and from there, Abraham completed his quest southward and landed in Canaan (modern-day Israel). It was amazing to be here in the midst of biblical history!

I found it surprising to find that there were many Russian people in Armenia. The Ukrainians were not the only ones fleeing their country. Many Russians were afraid of the war and possible retaliation by Ukraine, so there were many Russian refugees in Armenia. Once again, the people were not to blame. They thought everyone hated them. But remember that they too were displaced and needed a kind word, an encouraging touch, and a helping hand. It's God's command to us to love the refugee and the foreigner amongst us (Deuteronomy 10:19). True, I'm not from Armenia either, but I am a servant of the Most High. God is at work, although I cannot say how at this moment.

As we began a new production in the capital city of Yerevan with Pastors Artur and Armen, I could only imagine that the Lord had a collision course set for the Holy Spirit and for those in desperate need for a touch from God.

Am I supposed to be in Armenia? The Lord has a humorous way of confirming His call on our lives. Running errands here in town, I could see all the signs were written in Armenian. Suddenly, in the sea of Armenian signs, one was written boldly in English. The name of the shop? Montez! A clothing store. On the same day, we went in a grocery store to buy tea. The name of the preferred tea in Armenia? Richard! The box was blue and sported a lion. The Lion of Judah. I looked up and thanked the Lord quietly in the store. Like all other countries He'd sent me to, once again, He had confirmed my call to be in Armenia. My prayer was that once again, the Lord would use me. And once again, He heard my prayer. The show in the Middle East was a hit! The hall filled with thousands of people, and hundreds came to Christ gloriously. The show was once again a success. Artistically, yes. But more so because of the spiritual fruit that the drama produced. God made His presence known, and it was evident to everyone.

Such theatre events are what make my life so exhilarating. The five things that move my heart, the love of God, the love of seeing people know God, the love of people, the love of travel, and the love of theatre, suddenly all come together in a faraway country that proves that the Lord is present everywhere, ready to use anyone, including a little boy who once danced in the dark in an arid west Texas alley, to now move untold amounts of people around the world through theatre, directing each show as the man behind the curtain.

Chisenau, Moldova

EPILOGUE

After my work is done in a country, I arrive at the airport with my spirit focused on my new destination. It's always hard to say goodbye, but that's part of the ministry I've dedicated my life to. The Lord reminds me that there will be other needs, other shows, and other hellos to friends I've yet to meet.

I board the plane and feel the familiar power of the jet as it takes off, but I always feel a greater power blowing beneath the wings of my soul. As my plane departs, I reflect for a moment on my life's journey: From humble beginnings dancing in a dark alley to the stages of Disney, national theatres, stadiums, and even soccer fields that glorify God across the globe—I have been faithful to my God, who gives me strength. There have been many Goliaths in my life, but I have discovered that the David within me rises victoriously each time.

I close my eyes and wonder, *What horizon, what shore has He chosen for me this time?* I look out the window of the 747 that hurls me across His incredible creation to my next temporary home I've more than likely never been to before. My stage. My life. This is who I am, who I was created to be, working behind the scenes. My heart is filled with joy as I watch lives change from behind the curtain.

> *My heart, O God, is steadfast, my heart is steadfast, I will sing and make music.*
>
> —Psalm 57:7

ABOUT THE
AUTHOR

International Christian theatre director, Richard Montez, has led a successful theatre career in 101 countries for thirty-five years. He worked as a singer/dancer for Disneyland and was involved in all aspects of professional theatre before becoming a born-again Christian. *The Man Behind the Curtain* is taken from excerpts from a lifetime of journaling. Richard takes you on a journey of foreign lands, colorful theatrical productions, and unforgettable people, but ultimately, a God-led journey through the heart on how to discover God's gifts in you and to put them to use to impact the world.

Richard has enjoyed industry acclaim and artistic loyalty around the world. Now, he wants to share those adventures with everyone trying to find their calling and their purpose on earth.

Richard's shows have been translated into over twenty different languages, and he continues traveling directing shows in many foreign countries.

Richard uses his free time to write new shows, study God's Word, and write to draw others closer to the Lord through online Bible studies. Finally, he is the author of a Bible Study video series called "Journey to God," which can be found on the YouVersion Bible app.

CPSIA information can be obtained
at www.ICGtesting.com
Printed in the USA
LVHW081149141022
730656LV00013B/490